"If you have never cried while reading a book, this could be your first time. In *One Small Sparrow*, Jeff Leeland chronicles his then 10-month old son's struggle against a fatal bone marrow disease. With the ear of a poet, the heart of a dad, and the faith of a saint, he takes the reader through the medical torture his baby must endure to live…. Leeland's writing s[...]

KAREN S. PET[
USA TODAY, 15 M[

"I was deeply moved by this powe[...]
joy. If you need a reminder of the p[...]
possibilities of miracles, let this book touch you as well."

LEEZA GIBBONS
T.V. TALK SHOW HOST

"The most moving and heartrending story we have offered in the six years of our *Guidepost* condensed books program. Our readers loved it!"

TERRI CASTILLO,
GUIDEPOST SENIOR BOOK EDITOR

"I've been in a lot of hospitals over the past few years, and it breaks my heart to go into the children's wards. That has to be the worst time for any parent. What a blessing it would be for all of us to step in and help them at their point of need. I pray that God's people will help fund The Sparrow Foundation."

LARRY BURKETT,
CHRISTIAN FINANCIAL CONCEPTS, INC.

"*One Small Sparrow* will tear at your heart and remind you to slow down and consider the things that really matter. Put this book on the top of the stack—it's well worth your time!"

TERRY MEEUWSEN,
CO-HOST, *THE 700 CLUB*

"There is a healing that comes only through God's touch. There is another healing that comes only through others God uses to touch us. Finally, there is a healing that comes only when we share our stories. *One Small Sparrow* is about all these healings."

MICHAEL CARD

"*One Small Sparrow* is the story of a little boy who touched an entire TV newsroom and then a whole community. How wonderful that his story lives on in so many others!"

KATHI GOERTZEN,
KOMO TV NEWS ANCHOR, SEATTLE

"*One Small Sparrow* is one of the most moving stories I've ever read. Your tears will flow freely as it reminds you that even in the turmoil of today's society, God's love brings people together to give of themselves. The next time you sit down to read a good book, make it this one."

JACK ZIMMERMAN, PUBLISHER,
TODAY'S LIBRARIAN MAGAZINE

"Cancer touches us all. This is one family's journey, told in a unique, honest style. It is a story of the courage and hope of an entire community reaching out to help one of its own—a rarity these days. Jan and I were encouraged and challenged as we read *One Small Sparrow*. We trust you will be, too."

DAVE DRAVECKY

"You will not be able to put this book down. Many tears will be shed as you read this heartfelt story of what God's grace, community teamwork, and two parents determined to save their child can accomplish."

DON JAMES, FORMER HEAD FOOTBALL COACH,
UNIVERSITY OF WASHINGTON

"As one of Michael's physicians, I was enlightened by *One Small Sparrow*, which made me realize that the medical staff views only a fragment of a family's struggles. Many families who can relate wholeheartedly to Michael's story have benefited by knowing that other families have overcome similar adversities."

JULIE R. PARK, M.D., ASSISTANT PROFESSOR,
DEPARTMENT OF PEDIATRICS, UNIVERSITY OF WASHINGTON

"Each time you hear cancer being discussed with a family for the first time, you see the shock, disbelief, and fear in their eyes. You know only a little of the journey they must travel. This is the story of an entire community that banded together to say to one family, "You are not alone.""

CATHY ESTREMERA RN, PEDIATRIC ONCOLOGY NURSE MANAGER

"*One Small Sparrow* is a great read! I'm sure that you will agree with me after reading this inspiring story of victory. It will prompt you, too, to strain your "inner ear" to hear the voice of the Master and to respond to His urgings."

PAT CLEMENT

"Jeff Leeland goes right for the heart in *One Small Sparrow*. You are bound to be encouraged after reading this wonderful true story."

DR. DALE PARNELL, PROFESSOR EMERITUS,
OREGON STATE UNIVERSITY

"*One Small Sparrow* is not a book for the birds—it's an emotion-packed story for you about a little boy whose struggle impacted an entire community. Be sure to have a box of Kleenex handy!"

JOHN VAN DIEST, ASSOCIATE PUBLISHER,
MULTNOMAH PUBLISHERS, INC.

"*One Small Sparrow* will captivate your heart and lift your spirits as it draws you into the story of one family's struggle to save their little boy and of the community that came to their rescue. I wholeheartedly recommend you read this extraordinary book and that you buy copies for your friends as well!"

WALT KALLESTAD, COMMUNITY CHURCH OF JOY

"My listeners rank this book at the top of all the stories I've introduced on more than one thousand shows. It inspires; it empowers; it motivates—but, most of all, it proves that the living God makes His strength perfect in our weakness. I give copies of *One Small Sparrow* to those facing life's toughest struggles. Jeff Leeland offers us boundless hope to lift us above the 'what- ifs' and 'yes-buts' of our circumstances. This true story teaches us to say, "Count me down, but don't count me out!""

PHYLLIS WALLACE, HOST, *WOMAN TO WOMAN* RADIO SHOW AND
LUTHERAN HOUR MINISTRIES

"I was pleased that we were able to put this book in the hands of every FCA huddle coach in the country. I was so touched by *One Small Sparrow* that I wanted to give all of them the chance to replicate this model of love in their own communities. As you can see, our ministry is now part of "the rest of the story.""

ROD HANDLEY, SENIOR VICE-PRESIDENT,
FELLOWSHIP OF CHRISTIAN ATHLETES

"My son is a survivor of childhood cancer. From personal experience I know that life's most profound lessons are learned in the places of deepest sorrow and struggle. I also know that fields of exquisite, beautiful poppies grow only where the land has been "disturbed." In his book, Jeff graciously and powerfully recounts: his land disturbed—his sorrows experienced—his lessons learned. Come—see the beauty! Come—read what God does!!"

DEBORAH A. KLASSEN,

POPULAR CANADIAN SOLO MUSICAL ARTIST

"For all of us who think that some problems are just too big, *One Small Sparrow* is a passionate and wonderful reminder of the difference we can make when we ignore the odds and put our trust in our Creator."

GEOFF MOORE,

POPULAR CHRISTIAN RECORDING ARTIST

"*One Small Sparrow* is a wonderfully encouraging testament to God's graciousness and to the way that He moves in the hearts and minds of men, women, *and* children to bring real healing."

JOHN B. PRENTIS, PUBLISHER,

WORLD MAGAZINE

"When you need proof of God's love; when current events have made you angry or cynical; when you need something inspirational—read *One Small Sparrow*. You can probably read it in one sitting. But you'll also want to re-read this true story of God's love."

MARGARET O'CONNELL, ASSOCIATE EDITOR,

THE CHRISTOPHERS, NEW YORK, CATHOLIC NEWS SERVICE

"*One Small Sparrow* is a beautifully written, moving story from a father's heart about the good that can come out of tragedy when the love of God is expressed through compassionate people. This book is a powerful message to us all that we can make a difference in the world!

CHERI FULLER, AUTHOR OF *WHEN FAMILIES PRAY,*

WHEN CHILDREN PRAY, AND *WHEN MOTHER'S PRAY*

"Don't rush through this one! Take time to savor the myriad of blessings recorded in this little book. You will meet a young family struggling and a community sacrificing to save a little boy's life against all the odds."

VICTOR H. HANSON III,
BIRMINGHAM NEWS COMPANY

"In five years of covering dramatic stories for The 700 Club, I have never come across a more inspiring story than the Leelands'. In an age of violence, *One Small Sparrow* shows us how God can turn the most devastating situation into a miraculous blessing. In this time of school shootings, it shows us how He can take a group of energetic public school teenagers and use them to help save the life of a dying child."

GORMAN WOODFIN,
THE 700 CLUB, CBN PRODUCER

This book is dedicated to the little boy who, I pray,
will grow up to fulfill many visions of hope,
to recognize the price paid for him in love, and
to dedicate himself fully to repay his debt of love
to God and his fellow man.

Owe no one anything except to love one another.

ROMANS 13:8, NKJV

one small sparrow

Michael's Story
and the Hope of Compassion
in the Classroom

JEFF LEELAND

Multnomah® Publishers *Sisters, Oregon*

ONE SMALL SPARROW
published by Multnomah Publishers, Inc.

© 2000 by Jeff Leeland
International Standard Book Number: 1-57673-693-8

Cover design by Kirk DouPonce
Cover image by Photodisc

Scripture quotations are from:
The Holy Bible, New International Version (NIV) ©1973, 1984
by International Bible Society, used by permission of
Zondervan Publishing House

Also quoted:
The Holy Bible, New King James Version (NKJV)
©1984 by Thomas Nelson, Inc.

Multnomah is a trademark of Multnomah Publishers, Inc., and
is registered in the U.S. Patent and Trademark Office.
The colophon is a trademark of Multnomah Publishers, Inc.

Printed in the United States of America

For information:
MULTNOMAH PUBLISHERS, INC.
POST OFFICE BOX 1720
SISTERS, OREGON 97759

00 01 02 03 04 05 — 10 9 8 7 6 5 4 3 2 1 0

CONTENTS

Acknowledgments

Although it would better reflect my heart, acknowledging everyone responsible for Michael's story would be an insurmountable task. I can only hope that God has kept good accounts and, in His time, will fully give credit where credit is due. My purpose here is to acknowledge those whose aim was to get this story into print.

First, to my wonderful wife, Kristi, whose patient encouragement and painful recollecting helped mold the book, I love you.

To my children—Jaclyn, Amy, Kevin, Michael, and now Andrew—you are more precious than you can ever imagine. Now I can resume reading you bedtime stories instead of writing one.

To our close relatives and friends, your support and interest spurred me on in putting words to the song in my heart.

To Sealy Yates, your advocacy and efforts in ushering the manuscript forward is deeply appreciated.

To Don Jacobson, not only have I gained a most excellent publisher, but more importantly, I feel I've gained a brother and a friend.

To Jeff Gerke, Carol Bartley, and Steve Halliday, as editors you are true artists and faithful laborers. May your efforts in interviewing people and polishing the written words of a rough-edged coach reflect honorably upon you.

And finally to the Dameons and the sparrow-helpers and all those who give of themselves in the shadows of life and in the midst of personal adversity, never forget—there is a Sparrow Watcher.

His Eye Is on the Sparrow

Why should I feel discouraged,
When the shadows come?
Why should my heart be lonely,
And long for heaven and home,
When Jesus is my portion,
My constant friend is He…
His eye is on the sparrow.

Let not your heart be troubled.
His tender word I hear,
And resting on his goodness,
I lose my doubts and fears.
Though by the path He leadeth,
But one step I may see…
His eye is on the sparrow.

Whenever I am tempted,
Whenever clouds arise,
When song gives place to sighing,
When hope within me dies,
I draw the closer to Him,
From care He sets me free…
For His eye is on the sparrow,
And I know He watches me.

His eye is on the sparrow
And I know He watches me.
I sing because I'm happy,
I sing because I'm free.
For His eye is on the sparrow,
And I know He watches me.

CIVILLA D. MARTIN

FOREWORD
A Message to Young Readers

My students learned at least one thing from me: that I liked them. Maybe that's all they learned in my class—I hope not, but even if it is all they learned, that's not too bad. Deep down, maybe that's what they needed most. In their world of making grades and trying to look good and be popular and athletic, if just somebody at school, even a coach, liked them simply for being them, that would be a good thing.

And now you're reading my story. Welcome! I consider you to be one of my students, too. *One Small Sparrow* is a book for you—inspired in a big way by my students. Join me in my classroom on this difficult, but inspiring journey.

Let's begin.

The first lesson I learned on this journey was to face the truth. Even when facing the truth doesn't feel safe—like not wanting to know your baby has cancer—I learned it's better to accept the truth and adjust my life accordingly than to go on in false security. Truth needs a chance to pave the way inside us to real peace. Truth is an inner compass and a map of the way things really are. It guides us through the fog of uncertainty and difficulty.

Second, I learned to honestly *feel*. Facing truth can mean dealing with severe disappointment. It takes courage to feel afraid or deeply sad and not panic or do something foolish. When emotions overcome us like powerful waves, it's okay to cry—even for a guy. Teardrops, like ocean spray, come from the deepest parts of the ocean inside us. Mysteriously, my tears understand me. Emotions are good.

Third, I have learned compassion. Compassion changes my orientation—it's called a paradigm shift. I see my own problems from a different point of view. My eyes are opened to the broken sparrows around me—lowly, lonely, unnoticed people. Compassion can turn my self-pity into empathy. My hurts can teach me to care about others.

Compassion has become my classroom. And my best teachers have been hospitalized children who've held onto hope, disabled people who've overcome odds, forgotten grandpas and grandmas hidden away in old folks' homes who remember their loved ones often, unpopular kids in school who care about others. They give me keys to true treasures in my chest—my heart-gifts. And considering their burdens has made my own grow strangely lighter.

Fourth, I've learned I have powerful gifts inside me. The smallest hydrogen atom can trigger the most powerful nuclear chain reaction. Our heart-gifts—no matter how small and insignificant they may seem—can trigger an even greater chain reaction of good. May I never again underestimate the heroic power of one "powerless" person. No matter what I'm facing, I can choose to be a blessing. And by choosing to reach out and help, my heart grows wings and I rise above myself. Love overcomes fear.

Finally, I've learned there is a place for compassion in every classroom. We teachers have nourished your bodies and nurtured your brains, but your souls have been expelled from school. For fourteen years I've taught in public schools, but now my classroom has changed. It's called The Sparrow Foundation. We establish Sparrow Clubs—schools of compassion within every school, for every young person with an open heart. And the lessons are universal.

Chicken Soup for the Surviving Soul did a story about *One Small Sparrow* and called it, "Teens Launch Campaign to Save Dying Baby's Life." Not long after, I received a letter postmarked from Tehran, Iran. It was from a teacher who'd translated the story from English into Farsi (Iranian) for her students. Her response put wind under my wings.

> I would like to be of service to your Sparrow Foundation and will be very grateful to receive guidelines and advices from you...to enrich my knowledge and mental power to fight against despair—the cancer in my students which is much more dangerous than any illness.

May we all "fight against despair"—that deadly symptom of moral cancer. We need a transfusion of truth and hope. And we need donors of love who know they are loved. Final diagnosis—our culture cannot survive without it.

Read on, my student. In this classroom, there are no grades—just grace.

INTRODUCTION
Before the Beginning

K risti and her girlfriend went to the Fellowship of Christian Athletes banquet to hear and perhaps meet the guest speaker—a Seattle Seahawk, a strong man of faith who happened to play pro football.

My purpose for attending, I thought, was to hear this guy as well—until she walked in. My heart was instantly pierced by her steel gaze. And without thinking, I raised my hand like a white flag and waved.

I was won.

The Seahawk never had a chance to meet the prettiest girl in the room that night. In fact, he was clueless eight months later when this second-string Husky from the University of Washington pulled a giant upset over him.

On July 26, 1980, Kristi became my wife, Mrs. Jeff Leeland.

She was won.

The everyday storms that families face visited us soon after our vows. Our checkbook became one, too. An overdraft notice greeted us when we arrived home from our honeymoon. "Someone" with perfect addition credited the check for wedding flowers...instead of subtracting it. We discovered early on that even though humor won't keep the boat afloat, it does make the ride more fun.

Career decisions brought rough waters as well. Some might say we fit into that category of couples who had kids before they could "afford them." Possibly. Kristi had a good job when we were first married but gave it up to invest her time and energy into "little things." Since then we have done without the lesser things.

Our first big storm hit us soon after we purchased our first home and had our first child, Jaclyn. I was unexpectedly laid off, along with seventy-five other educators, from a large, suburban, Seattle school district. The ax usually falls at the bottom of the totem pole—and that's exactly where I was in my first year of teaching.

A feverish statewide job search that summer of 1982 finally landed Kristi, Jaclyn, and me on the sunny side of the Cascade Mountains in the rural, wide open spaces of Eastern Washington. I became the physical education teacher and a football coach at Omak High School. Never heard of Omak, Washington? Likely not, unless you are a fan of the famous Stampede Rodeo and Suicide Race.

Over the next several years that little town of Omak grew on us as much as our family grew in it. We bought an old, little two-bedroom house that we fixed up. Then came Amy. Then came Kevin. Then we bought a hide-a-bed for the living room where Kristi and I slept for the next two years. It was cozy. We were happy. God was good.

In the wash of those eleven years there were a couple more moves and an urge within me to do something different. I considered other career opportunities, possibly school administration, perhaps counseling. I took college extension courses. We trusted that doors would open when the time was right, but we were not anxious to leave our little town.

January, 1991. The new year began with a joyous blessing. Kristi had a certain knack for not being able to bottle up the living secret she treasured inside her.

And here Michael's story truly begins.

Chapter One

NEW BEGINNINGS

A ugust 19, 1991. I sit in a hospital room with the TV on, oblivious to the reporter's sense of urgency regarding incidents taking place halfway around the world.

"A military takeover in the Soviet Union…" drones the reporter, competing with the news of a baby born in Omak, Washington. No doubt about it, though. All that matters to me today is Michael Jeffrey Leeland.

Michael—the blond-haired, blue-eyed boy whom Kristi has prayed for. He is the next link in our family of Jaclyn, age nine; Amy, age six; and Kevin, age three. Born by C-section, Michael will cause Kristi's recovery to be much slower this time.

My heart sinks with the long distance phone call. The new teaching position at Kamiakin Junior High in Seattle is offered to me. The promise we made weeks earlier to accept the job under certain circumstances now confronts us at this inopportune time. Should we renege, try to back out gracefully? What before seemed like a great opportunity now feels like a burden.

On the other hand, a violated conscience would be a greater burden. The bottom line: We gave our word we would accept the offer if the principal at Kamiakin could arrange a full-time position and the Omak School District could find a replacement for me.

The probability of both happening only a week before the start of school seemed very unlikely. Now, to our dismay, the pieces of this puzzle are falling into place on the very day Michael is born!

Thoughts of moving halfway across the state of Washington depress us. Combined stressors of

    a new baby,

        Kristi's surgery,

           my absence from home,

               adjusting to a new job,

                   finding a place to live,

                      packing,

                          moving to a new community…

occurring all at once are simply overwhelming.

Nevertheless, we take a step of faith. Our decision must go beyond plusses and minuses to honor and integrity. Reluctantly we decide to move away from Omak to Seattle, hoping and praying we are doing the right thing—if not the comfortable thing.

August 26. I forge out ahead of my family to start the new job. As I back out of the driveway, I wave goodbye to Kristi and the kids. Heaviness grips my heart like an iron vise, and tears fill my eyes.

Looking ahead to the long drive to Seattle and to an uncertain future makes it even harder to leave. As I travel down the road, I wonder, "Is this a big mistake? Is it too late to turn around?"

My hectic schedule in the first three weeks of September

keeps me from dwelling on the ache I feel below the surface, but there it is. The family-shaped void of relationship deep inside leaves a painfully empty feeling. I struggle with loneliness. But the roles of junior high athletic director, activities coordinator, teacher, and coach allow no time to wallow in self-pity as I labor to keep my head above water.

I become a weekend commuter. Friday afternoon: four and a half hours of joyful anticipation as I drive home to my family in Omak. Sunday afternoon: four and a half hours of hollow anxiety as I drive back to work in Seattle.

Until September 20!

We move 270 miles to our new home in Bothell, Washington, a Seattle suburb ten miles from school. A family again!

At last we enjoy a Sunday afternoon with hearts left intact. We have learned through the weeks of separation many valuable lessons of appreciation. Perhaps the biggest: never take one another for granted. New baby, new job, new home, new community—all give us much to look forward to.

Chapter Two

SECOND THOUGHTS

Strange how feelings of isolation and disconnectedness can strike hard even while surrounded by hordes of people. How can city dwellers live side-by-side for months, years, without finding ties or emotional links even to their neighbors?

In early January, four months after our move, Kristi and I sit on the kitchen floor,

> reminiscing,
>> rehashing,
>>> sharing a case of "mover's remorse."

"Why are we here, Lord?"

We long for the intimacy of small-town living again. Omak, our home for ten years, featured neighborly neighbors, a two-bedroom house for twenty-three thousand dollars, and a daily stop at the post office for our mail. It's a rural community of five thousand and the birthplace of Amy, Kevin, and Michael. Omak boasts the only stoplight in Okanogan County (whether needed or not). My daily commute consisted of a two-block walk to work and a walk home for lunch.

Yeah, believe it or not, we miss it.

Back in the city now after ten years of being away, we get this sense of "urban aloofness," where rubbing lots of elbows gets you awfully cold shoulders. Seattle is a place of freeway driving, kamikaze commuters, and the unwritten rule of the urban road: "Nice guys get there last."

It's quite different in the small community. There you have a thing called a "reputation," something that follows you around and helps keep you honest (or at least semipolite). I sometimes think people move to the city to escape the reputation they earned in a small town. It's easier to hide in the city.

We're still getting the Omak *Chronicle,* the small-town, weekly newspaper. It's like a fresh, country breeze which briefly pushes aside the smoggy, metropolitan haze.

What's the attraction of the little rag? First, a noticeable void of sensational, bad news. Such a void is typically filled with columns about ordinary, everyday people doing ordinary, everyday things extraordinarily well. Or maybe with something about last week's weather. Oh, there's also no pollution index.

Boring? Maybe. But better a little boredom from lack of sensationalism than complete callousness from too much. At least with deprivation, there is hope!

We miss the simple, reflective way of life. Sure, Omak doesn't have all the conveniences of Seattle, but strong relationships, like good character, seem to be nourished by inconvenience. And yes, there is something down-to-earth about the small-town way, where you won't see people riding elevators up to fifth-floor health clubs to use the latest "stair stepper" machines.

City life moves in the left lane—much faster, more complicated, and far more impersonal. There are tons of things to do, more things to have, and far less time to simply be.

So we find ourselves sitting here on the kitchen floor, maybe experiencing the "little fish in a big pond" syndrome. Our roots are having trouble finding depth in the asphalt jungle. Perhaps we have just a touch of the January blues.

For whatever reason, we feel a little depressed and wonder how things would be different had we stayed in Omak.

Chapter Three

FIRST ALERT

Wednesday, January 15, 2:15 A.M. From our bed I hear the cries of baby Michael. His cry is unusual and definitely off schedule.

"Kristi, Michael's awake."

I must confess, husbands of nursing mothers become a bit complacent about cries in the night. But only minutes later I'm slapped in the face by Kristi's words: "Jeff, Michael's got a high fever."

Surprises connected with children keep life—and sleep—from happening in efficient, neatly wrapped, little packages. There's no such thing as tight organization when our lives become so intimately linked with these little people.

"How high?" I ask, jumping out of the sack.

"It's 103.5 degrees."

"I'd better get the Tylenol."

"I'll call the clinic in the morning."

Since Michael is our fourth child, umpteen kid fevers have preceded this one. We know the protocol.

That evening as I am coming home from a night class after school, I wonder how Michael's appointment went. I arrive home, walk in the door and greet Kristi, and immediately sense something is wrong.

"How's Michael?"

The words spill from her heart, "He had a spinal tap."

Tears well up in her eyes.

"What's the matter?" I ask with rising apprehension.

"They did a blood test—his white count is really high. The doctor thought he might have spinal meningitis."

"What did they find?"

"The test was negative. She thinks Michael must have some other kind of infection. He's on antibiotics."

"So…he'll be okay?"

"Yeah," she responds, again with tears. "He cried so hard when they put that needle in his back." She goes on to describe holding Michael still while the doctors took their sample.

We are both relieved it's over. We assume it's over…until a worsening cough, a congested chest, and the return of Michael's fever five days later signal otherwise. With each breath his skin retracts between his small ribs.

The pediatric clinic, a pit stop in our race to get help, validates our fear; X-rays show Michael has pneumonia.

Twenty minutes later we arrive at Children's Hospital in Seattle. The emergency room is packed with lots of other sick kids and nurses cursing the month of January. It's flu season.

Michael is admitted, vital signs and blood tests are taken, an IV is set up, and he's finally in a room by ten that evening.

Chapter Four

SEEDS OF SUFFERING

January 21. Michael shares a room with Jake, a struggling one-year-old with viral pneumonia and a struggling single mother. He works for every breath. He gasps out his cries, innocent little eyes asking why.

Michael and Jake are continuously monitored, wired for heart rate and blood oxygen levels. With each heartbeat a new mountain peak and valley cross the range of the computer screen. With each pulse a new reading of oxygen levels: 90 percent...88 percent...86 percent...90 percent.... This moment-by-moment medical technology provides objective data to be objectively interpreted by objective caregivers. The lower the blood oxygen, the higher the heart rate. A causal, not casual, relationship.

To the parent hovering alongside the sick one, each heartbeat is a peak and valley of emotion, a roller coaster of hope and fear. "Spread out, peaks! Slow down, heart! You're working much too hard. Go up, oxygen!" This is an intimate relationship.

Eventually, anxiety gives way to prayer, exhaustion to sleep.

And...our hopes and prayers are answered. Michael

responds rapidly to treatment and is released to go home the next evening, January 22.

Oddly, just before discharging Michael, the young resident doctor finds something peculiar about Michael's platelets, the clotting cells in his blood. Counts normally register between 200,000 and 300,000 platelets; Michael's level is only 70,000. Also, the infection-fighting, white cells are still abnormally high at 40,000; typical range is 7,000 to 10,000.

Seeming curious but not alarmed, the doctor requests weekly follow-up tests at our pediatric clinic.

"Blood counts can easily be thrown off by pneumonia and fever," he reassures us, tempering our concern. We appreciate his thoroughness and are thankful to take Michael home.

The following month brings weekly visits to Michael's pediatrician for simple blood tests. Three weeks pass without any reappearance of his illnesses, yet the abnormalities in his counts stubbornly remain.

On February 17 we are referred to the specialists at Children's Hospital and Medical Center in Seattle. The sign over the door reads "Hematology/Oncology." It's Greek to me. All we know is they will soon be getting at the root of Michael's abnormal blood counts by taking a sample of bone marrow.

Seated in the waiting room, I am touched as a pretty little girl hobbles in on crutches. There are no broken bones. The only sign of the disease hides under her pink, polka-dotted bonnet. Her bald little head is a pitiable sight. *Doesn't cancer treatment do that to hair?* I wonder. Her mother sits nearby with an air of calm gentleness, like a seasoned veteran tried in the fires of a tremendous battle.

Kristi feels the weight of her heart moving her to ask, "How is your little girl doing?" I listen in. A tumor. Cancer. The prescribed regimen: chemotherapy, radiation, surgery. Then therapy once more and learning to walk again.

So young,
  so innocent,
    so tragic.

At least for now she is in recovery. In her mother's eyes there is hope, and courage.

But in our hearts, there is brokenness and fear. Thoughts of "what if...?" flood my mind. For the first time I draw a link between Michael's blood and the rare possibility of cancer.

Immediately I am compelled to be with my son, so I knock on the examination room door, both unaware of and unconcerned with clinic rules and procedures. I care only about the sound of my baby crying—the result of another long needle, this time piercing his pelvic bone.

Doctors finish the bone marrow aspiration just in time for me to hold and comfort Michael. All I can think is, "Everything will be okay. We love you, Michael. Dear God, be with Michael!"

Thus begins a season of
  waiting,
    hoping,
      praying,
far more intense than ever before.

The results of the test will not be known for at least a week.

Chapter Five

WHAT IF?

We have been living nine days in an emotional casino, waiting for results of Michael's tests. We find daily strength has little to do with knowledge, much to do with belief. Hopes rest either in medical percentages, blind luck, or faith in God. After a struggle, objectivity and passion become reconciled in a parent's heart.

In scientific terms: symptoms, medical data, diagnoses. Questions, tests, trial and error, protocols. Cold, hard, objective data. Medical science thrives on questions.

In parental terms: a warm, precious baby. Questions, uncertainty, anxiety. Symptoms, possibilities, hopes, and fears. A mother and father long for answers, wait and pray for answers, to Michael's tests.

"What if Michael has leukemia?"

Our deepest fear remains unspoken. "Don't even mention the word! He looks so good—a happy little boy. Things are back to normal now. He looks so healthy! Keep busy. Don't worry. Take life as usual. Try not to think about it. Think positive!" We dodge the "what if" question and energetically engage in mental gymnastics and denial.

It's hard work not to think about something so vital, so

threatened. We strive to be consciously unconscious. But moments of solitude and reflection draw to the surface even our inmost thoughts.

"What if...?"

Reality. Vulnerability. Love and pain made inseparable by truth.

How badly we want Michael to be well! What can we do? Should we act this way, think these things? "Say this. Don't say that!" There must be something we can or should do that might influence the outcome.

We find ourselves desperate to be in control, yet we know this is the root of vain superstition. How does a parent reconcile this driving passion to care for a child with the reality of human limits? The lines seem very fine between legitimate concern and harmful worry, between release to God and irresponsible denial. It is a distinction that has everything to do with the character of one's God.

Is God really adequate? Does He personally care? Am I willing simply to trust and obey Him, willing to risk knowing Him better?

Finally, the waiting comes to an end.

Wednesday, February 26, 1992. Usual routines start my day. Get up at six, shower, dress, eat a bowl of oatmeal, and have a quiet time before I leave for work. I spend a special time in prayer for Michael. Our God makes the difference.

Later that morning the clock on my office wall prompts me to think about Michael's bone marrow test. My enforced pace slows enough for me to face once again the gravity of this matter.

Ten o'clock. Is there any news? Time to call home. A biggie.

"Hello, sweetheart....What's wrong?"

Chapter Six

WHY MICHAEL?

"Michael has what?" I ask, hardly comprehending Kristi's words. Dr. Park had called just moments before. "Myelo what?"

Through tears, Kristi repeats the diagnosis: "Michael has myelodysplastic syndrome."

"What is that?"

"A type of leukemia." On the other end of the line, the voice breaks as a mother struggles for composure. "He needs a bone marrow transplant."

Two words, *leukemia* and *transplant,* combine into a sledgehammer punch to my gut. The idea rocks me on my heels.

Cancer. Terminal cancer. An unspoken terror of every parent. The shock leaves me groping for words, yet desperate for information.

What? How? When?

Instinctively I pull out the Post-its and scribble notes as Kristi talks:

- myelodysplastic syndrome
- monosome (half chromosome missing)

- preleukemia
- will not go away
- must treat eventually with bone marrow transplant
- Dr. Julie Park
- 9 A.M.—HLA markers (donors)

The appointment next week will start the donor search and answer more questions.

Alone, in silence, and suffering the heartache of crushing fear, my deepest question is simply why? Why Michael? This precious, innocent, baby boy. What has he done to deserve this? Why not the child abuser, the drug pusher, the criminal?

Why not me?

Such questions of the human heart challenge the adequacy of science alone to deeply satisfy. Answers must come by faith—a faith in our case now shaken to the foundation.

God, are You still there? Do You still love us? Are You still in control? How can this be?

And if my finger of blame points upward, three more aim right back at me. Could I have genetically passed this to my son? Did we blindly expose him to an environmental risk? Can I say my heart is pure, that I am above divine chastening?

For the deep questions there are no audible, easy answers. There are no heavenly visions, no angelic visitations, no instant, pain-relieving words of advice. In the depths of such doubt we feel only the certainty of sorrow.

An Interview With
Kristi Leeland
Kristi is Michael's mom.

"I had taken some classes at Edmonds Community College to become a medical assistant, so I knew what Michael might be facing as time went on. I had followed a patient at the University of Washington's oncology clinic, a guy about my age. So when they sent us to hematology/oncology, I knew what that could mean, but I thought, 'No, he doesn't have this.'

"When they finally identified Michael's problem and told us he needed a bone marrow transplant, it was like somebody took a baseball bat and hit me right across the forehead. I had just put down the phone from speaking to the doctor—I hadn't even taken my hand off the receiver—when Jeff called. I was sobbing and had a hard time talking to him."

Chapter Seven

DISCOVERING A
TIME BOMB

February 27. The devastating nature of Michael's disease becomes evident this very first day after the call. Spiking a high fever and developing a worsening cough and congested chest, Michael is again admitted to the hospital with pneumonia.

New battle lines are quickly drawn; the dreaded enemy has been discovered. Our family pediatrician will no longer be Michael's primary doctor. The hematologists/oncologists, specialists in childhood blood disease and cancer, now become Michael's caregivers at Children's Hospital in Seattle.

A new plan of attack is mapped out. The search for a bone marrow donor will begin in our family and, we hope, end with a rare and precious match.

Routine weekly blood tests and checkups must continue. If he gets a fever above 101.5°, Michael must immediately come to Children's Hospital. If his blood counts drop, he will be transfused with either red blood cells or platelets.

Ultimately the question of when the transplant must occur can be answered only by periodic tests of Michael's marrow. The art and science of timing is a huge part of this delicate medical procedure. Delaying a transplant too long means risking unremissible leukemia, complete bone marrow failure, or deadly infection. Rushing a transplant means risking irreversible toxic damage to a baby's little body.

Amazing things are happening in Michael's first year of life:
a developing pituitary gland,
a rapidly growing brain,
maturing little organs.

All are priceless cargo to carry through the transplant gauntlet of radical chemotherapy and radiation.

Will he really need a bone marrow transplant? Maybe something will change. If not, the longer he can wait, the better.

For now, his pneumonia means he must undergo another four-day hospital stay.

February 28. On a merry-go-round of hope and despair, I grasp for a small ring of control. Knowledge is the key! Uncertainty fueled by medical ignorance drives me to the Health Sciences Library at the nearby University of Washington. Being an alum gives me a slight acquaintance and remembrance of its resources.

What exactly is this rare and deadly disease hiding in Michael's bones? First stop, the Infotrac computer.

What incredible technology! Simply type in a word—*myelodysplastic*—push "return," and see a definition instantly displayed:

- myelo—originating within the bone marrow
- dysplastic—defective formation of cells

Vocabulary, the building blocks of intelligence. Well, what about *myelodysplastic*? I want more information, so I push another button. Instantly up-to-date summaries, abstracts, and research on any topic of choice pop onto the screen.

First article: "The myelodysplastic syndrome: kills through cytopenia or malignant transformation," by D. A. G. Galton, v. 299, *British Medical Journal*, Sept. 2, '89 p. 582.

I know *malignant* means cancer, but what in the world is *cytopenia?*

I type in *cytopenia*, and the screen immediately informs me: "decrease of cell elements in the blood." So that's why Michael's platelet and red blood cell counts are dropping!

I keep going, now with a voracious appetite for more input. What about *myelodysplastic syndrome?*

- characterized by overproduction of blood stem cells (the root cells of all blood);
- irregular growth of bone marrow cells;
- cells defective in structure and function;
- rare in people under the age of fifty;
- the syndrome is fatal.

My heart sinks into my stomach, but I am not finished reading. "Survival ranges from only weeks to years."

Things seem to sink in deeper when you read them in print. My fears reinforced, I search for new evidence to draw different conclusions. Could there possibly be a less severe course of treatment for Michael?

I read on and come across another abstract:

- various treatments used with little success;
- infections account for 64 percent of deaths before onset of acute leukemia.

No wonder the doctors are so aggressively treating Michael's fever and cough! The disease is like a time bomb ticking away inside his small body.

A new article: "Bone marrow transplant may provide cure, especially in younger patients who have recently developed the disease."

The curtain now slowly rises on the behind-the-scenes staging of this true-life drama. Only weeks earlier Kristi and I had sat on the kitchen floor wondering, "Lord, why did You bring us here?" and regretting the move to Seattle.

My thoughts of "what if" return, now in grateful retrospect. What if we had stayed in Omak? What if we had turned our backs on that uncomfortable commitment to a job change and instead had taken the path of least resistance? What if a small-town, family doctor had failed to recognize the warning signs of Michael's rare disease?

Even if Michael had been accurately diagnosed, he would have been sent to Children's Hospital in Seattle, which serves kids with cancer throughout the Pacific Northwest. It would have been Michael's home away from home, separating our family by hundreds of miles.

And what about the bone marrow transplant? The famous Fred Hutchinson Cancer Research Center in Seattle—pioneers and perfecters of the bone marrow transplant who are doing more in this area than any other hospital in the world—are now in our own backyard! There is no better place for our baby to be.

We are humbled by the grace, awed by the divine orchestration of events. We can only pray. "Dear God, thank You for divinely transplanting our family from Omak to Seattle."

Chapter Eight

HOSPITAL HALLWAYS

It's early March. I enter Children's Hospital and pass by a child struggling to walk, a young boy sporting braces on both legs. How can I forget the determined look in his eyes? His misfortune, in a moment's glance, is my inspiration. His condition floods my heart with compassion.

Never to romp in backyard games, never to hear the cheers of sporting fans, never to score for the home team—but this boy hits a home run in my heart. A better victory is won in the heart.

No Super Bowl will ever match this single moment of a young, crippled boy's effort. These children with incredible innocence daily face pain and adversity with utter dignity and courage, turning tragedy into triumph, striking chords of passion, sounding the depths of heart and soul.

And where are the real life trophies? Rows and rows of plaques on the walls, lining the fifth floor hallway of Children's Hospital, bear the names of little ones—now memories only.

The inconceivable thought of losing our baby makes us fearfully avoid this normal pathway to the cafeteria. The fourth floor offers a far less threatening route. Why not go around these uncomfortable feelings?

The issue of ultimate ownership and control is something every parent must face when walking this pathway. Who is our child's true Father? Could God love Michael more than we do? Can we accept the role of temporal guardians with faithful and grateful hearts?

And so we take trembling steps of faith down this corridor, entrusting our child into the loving hands of God. We gain what we can never lose by giving up what we cannot possess. And gradually we gain the assurance of God's grip on Michael no matter how helplessly loose ours may become.

And so we walk these hospital hallways free to
   love,
      enjoy,
         and emotionally cuddle
this little one on loan from heaven—knowing there are Everlasting Arms beneath him.

An Interview With
Dave and Jill Swenson

*Dave was one of Jeff's roommates in college and
has served as the Leelands' pastor at
Community Christian Fellowship in Edmonds.*

"I remember a Sunday afternoon phone call," says Dave. "When I heard of the severity of the situation, I was overwhelmed with an incredible sense of sadness. I have to say I wasn't very optimistic at that point. I thought, 'If I lost one of my children, it would be like ripping my heart out.' I think that emotional response on my part bonded Jeff and me together in a unique way.

"As a pastor, I try not to get too preachy. Although Scripture is our foundation, I don't want to just say, 'Here are seventeen Bible verses. Meditate on them and you'll feel better.' Sometimes silence is a ministry, an arm around someone, praying together, or just nodding and listening.

"I remember the night four or five couples were sitting in the living room and the Leelands walked in," Jill recalls. "We stopped to have an update. We all just cried and cried and cried. No one said anything; we didn't tell them, 'It's okay. Nothing's going to happen' or 'God's with you.' And then Jeff and Kristi talked about what God was doing in their lives. It was as if they were borne up on prayers and angels' wings."

Chapter Nine

A TEACHABLE MOMENT

The curiosity of children. They must ask three hundred questions a week—sometimes by ten o'clock Monday morning.

As we drive down the freeway, nine-year-old Jaclyn asks, "Dad, what's wrong with Michael?"

Children—both students and little sponges.

I recognize this as a teachable moment, an opportunity to be seized. "Well, honey, it's kind of like this freeway."

Parents—both teachers and pools. In my case, I hope a deep pool with a shallow end where little questions (and questioners) feel safe. My task is to paint pictures with words, to build bridges between familiar and unfamiliar territories. I must connect the profound to the simple.

I take a deep breath and give my answer.

"You see, Jaclyn, inside of you and me and Michael are miles and miles of highways called blood vessels. In those blood vessels travel millions and millions of tiny cars and trucks called blood cells. They go back and forth to work in the body and do different kinds of jobs. The factories that make those blood cells are inside our bones and are called bone marrow stem cells.

"Those factories make three different types of 'cars' or blood cells. The main type is red blood cells. Their job is to deliver oxygen to all other cells. The next type is platelets. Their job is to repair the highways, the vessels, by stopping bleeding. The last type is the white blood cells. Their job is to be the police by killing enemy infections.

"For some unknown reason, the cell factories inside the bones can start making mistakes. They leave out parts in the cells or make them wrong. Because the cells aren't finished, the factories can make lots of them really fast, but they don't work right. So they end up in a blood cell junkyard in two organs called the liver and spleen. They also start clogging up inside the bone marrow.

"After a while these bad factories and cells in the bone marrow take up all the space. As the good factories have less and less room to work, they produce fewer and fewer good cells. That means less oxygen is delivered, fewer blood vessels get repaired, and fewer infections are stopped. Then it is hard for the person to live anymore."

After a pause I say, "Jaclyn, Michael has bad factories."

The heart of the matter.

"Oh," says Jaclyn, quietly absorbing the pain.

Siblings of cancer patients are often left out of the loop by parents without

    enough time,

      enough energy,

        enough resources.

And hurting parents with human limits tend to create brothers and sisters without answers, without emotional support, without mom and dad—hurting siblings who wind up with tons of unmet needs.

Kristi and I determined at the outset that we would strive to be aware of our children's needs. Now putting words to the feelings of Jaclyn, Amy, and Kevin seems as important to their emotional health as defining Michael's illness was to his physical health. We all deeply long to be understood.

Our cry is simple: "We need help, Lord!"

A NEEDLE
IN A HAYSTACK

T he long and the short of it is this:

- no suitable donor, no transplant;
- no transplant, no hope (medically speaking) for Michael.

The immediate family spends an hour at the clinic, giving our blood for baby Michael. Samples for histocompatibility tests are taken in search of the perfect, six-out-of-six, bone marrow antigen match. It's a complex puzzle of compatibility.

Antigens are the genetic "fingerprints" of the immune system. Six discriminating detectives on each microscopic "warrior" white cell are given the task of discerning friends and foes throughout the body. If they recognize a friend, their job is to protect and defend. If a stranger is identified, it's a fight to the death.

Risking a mismatched transplant is like letting foxes guard the henhouse. Transplanted white cells attack the host's body, causing GVHD (graft-versus-host disease), a life-threatening complication.

Even in a "perfect," six-out-of-six match, there is still the risk of rejection, albeit less deadly. The mysterious human cell still hides many secrets from science. Medical technology, in a never-ending game of cat and mouse, corrects and recorrects and may reduce its margins of error, but it's never errorless.

Finding a match is another game of chance. The best hope doctors can give rests in medical statistics. The probability of finding a perfect match among siblings: one in four. Outside of the family, in the general population, it is like finding a needle in a haystack. The odds are one in twenty thousand.

Michael's advantage: the blessing of a brother and two sisters!

Now we are even more thankful as parents that we broke the national average of 1.5 children per household, despite the frequent comment, "Are all these yours?"

We have arrived at a new season of
> waiting,
>> hoping,
>>> praying
to the One who chuckles at impossible odds.

Chapter Eleven

REVOLVING DOORS

I f you stop on Floor 3 of Children's Hospital and exit the elevator to the left into Cluster A, you'll find the infant unit—tiny preemies fighting for life. Exit to the right into Cluster B, and you'll find kids with cancer. It's a bright and cheery place—homey, even—filled with hope and love.

A waiting room lies between Clusters A and B. Here you will find parents from all over the Northwest—Washington, Alaska, Idaho, Montana. Parents watch over the unit by day and sleep at the Ronald McDonald House by night. The parents of preemies and cancer patients share a like passion: They all carry an emotional burden for a precious little one. Black, white, Hispanic, Asian, rich, poor—all are brought together in the grip of pain. External barriers crumble in a waiting room.

Three-B is a special battlefield. A place where love rarely goes without saying, where courage and endurance are dominant themes. A place where children must undergo chemotherapy, a most toxic cure. Bags of toxic liquid are attached to an IV machine designed to pump the potent chemicals into the child's bloodstream. The noxious potion targets fast-dividing cancer cells, but attacks fast-dividing normal cells just as surely.

Hair cells are fast dividing. Mucus membrane is fast dividing. They are among the first to go. With cancer, better to overkill than to underkill. Hair and mucus can grow back.

Some kids on 3B, like Michael, need help against infection. Children with compromised immune systems are at high risk with abnormal blood counts. Powerful antibiotics and blood transfusions provide only a band-aid for children with leukemia, whose white cells are working improperly.

Since Michael's diagnosis in February we've lived a recurring nightmare. Michael coughs in the middle of the night, signaling another fever. We call and are instructed to bring him right to the emergency room.

I usually take Michael in. It's so difficult for Kristi to watch them do another IV on her baby. The kids also do better with Mom in the morning. When they wake up, Dad has gone again with their little brother. Grandma Leeland will likely come to stay with them during the day. Grandmas and grandpas have that special way about them that takes rough edges off hard things.

As I drive Michael away from home on the abandoned streets of Seattle, again en route to Children's, I assume Kristi has gone back to bed. But as soon as she kisses us good-bye, she quietly, routinely, kneels down beside our bed. In silent prayer she softly petitions her Savior. "Dear God, please keep Jeff awake at the wheel. Please keep Michael from being hospitalized. Please don't let this infection take his life...."

This morning is no different. Kristi prays...and later awakens, disoriented, still beside the bed, her head still resting on folded arms, her legs bent underneath her, numb with sleep.

Three-B. We are again in an isolated room. Pneumonia,

chicken pox—Michael, now eight months old, is caught in a revolving door. He spends twenty-one days hospitalized, mixed with fifteen days at home.

Our world has turned upside down. Home, work, hospital—a juggling act. Who will stay with Michael tonight? Who will watch our kids tomorrow? Will I need to call a sub for school?

We desperately try not to alienate Jaclyn, Amy, and Kevin. I try my best not to put a burden on my coworkers. I don't want to empower my weaknesses, to make excuses for getting behind in the minutia of a thousand other things to do.

But because I know Michael is a big enough reason to shift my priorities, I forfeit the rat race.

We have entered a world where the word "normal" does not refer to everyday life but to clinical routines: vital signs, medications, IVs, blood tests.

Today, yet another hospital stay with Michael on intravenous antibiotics; he's developing another worn-out, collapsed blood vessel. My job is to hold my son down while doctors and nurses try and try and try and try to puncture another vein to replace Michael's IV.

I tolerate the procedure with objective toughness only by knowing the good purpose to follow. I watch puncture after unsuccessful puncture into Michael's arms and legs.

Finally, in a glance my little boy's teary eyes speak to mine: "Daddy, Daddy—help!"

In a moment, volumes are communicated without a single word. How mighty are the eyes of a suffering child! What is in this penetrating vision that so deeply stirs my soul? Could it be in these little eyes I see a reflection of my own Father-longing?

"Daddy, Daddy—help!"

"Stop! That's enough!" I command the doctor as I pull my little one near.

A child is picked up in the loving arms of his father. A child finds comfort. A father is deeply pleased to comfort his child.

But will we take the risk of facing our pain, a pain that would drive us to a Father who cares?

Chapter Twelve

A LIGHT IN THE
DARKNESS

A phone call comes to me at school the morning of March 20. An elated voice cries out, "Amy is a perfect match!"

Kristi relays the information from Dr. Park—a related donor, a perfect, six-out-of-six match. It's the best possible scenario.

And our first taste of tangible hope for Michael.

"Thank you, Lord. Thank you!"

Amy—our bright and vivacious little six-year-old girl with fine, blond hair and striking dark brown eyes.

Michael—identical to Amy in so many ways. A sister and little brother whose rare bone marrow match will cement a bond for life.

Will she really understand what she'll be asked to do? How does one explain a bone marrow transplant to a six-year-old?

"Amy, after they take away Michael's bad blood cells that make him sick, you can give him some of your good cells to make him better."

Amy's response: "Will it hurt?"

"You will be asleep, so you won't feel anything. But then

it will hurt for a little while after. They'll keep you in the hospital and help you feel better in a few days."

Amy readily accepts her special role. She is more than willing to share her life to spare the life of her baby brother. In her words, she is able to do "what nobody else couldn't." She cheerfully spreads the good news to everyone—"Guess what! I'm a match!"

There are no sibling rivalries with Jaclyn and Kevin on this issue. With limited understanding, they too are happy Amy can help Michael.

Amy, the child who joyfully bounces through life impulsively spending her allowance to buy things for other people, who gives as naturally as she breathes.

But as time goes on, she is also a little girl who grows strangely quiet and reserved about this, preferring that we avoid the subject. We sense our Amy is becoming either unusually uncomfortable with attention or is afraid. A child who does not totally understand the process, yet she is willing still.

An Interview With
Dorothy Leeland
*Dorothy, Jeff's mother, lives in Edmonds,
a Seattle suburb.*

"We were on vacation in Arizona visiting another son and his family when we first heard about Michael," says Dorothy. "We didn't know at that point what the bone marrow transplant might cost or how difficult it would be. We just realized how important it was to get a good match. I was at Jeff's house when the results from the blood tests came back. Amy came bounding in, saying, 'Grandma, I'm compatible!'

"I took Michael into X-ray one time. You couldn't be right there, but you could see him. They had his arms strung up high, and you just wanted to go rescue him. It was painful to see the little guy suffer. But he was an unbelievably good patient. Just for the moment he was suffering, and then he'd be a happy baby again."

Chapter Thirteen

AN OMINOUS CLOUD

Unexpectedly, however, as a result of the donor search, a dark cloud casts its shadow over this hope. Kristi receives a phone call one afternoon which puzzles her.

"There's a problem with your insurance company," states the administrative voice bluntly. "You need to review your policy on transplant coverage." The patient financial office has run into red tape with our insurance carrier.

Kristi calls and relays the message to me at school.

"Of course we have insurance coverage on this!" I protest. "They've paid for everything for Michael so far." I know we have been covered by health insurance every moment since my job change from Omak.

I arrive home after school with one intent: dig out that policy. With more than a hint of disgust, I think, "It just can't be easy."

Kristi elaborates on her phone conversation as I feverishly flip through the pages of the thick booklet I had received after signing up for coverage last October. Finally after bumping my way through a maze of insurance jargon, I come across one short sentence in the "wayback" of our policy: a twelve-month waiting period on benefits related to organ transplants. We've only been here six months.

The large print giveth, the small print apparently taketh away!

Then I reason, *But Michael needs a bone marrow transplant. Can bone marrow even be considered an organ?* I hustle to the bookcase for our *World Book* dictionary and turn to organ: "3. any part of an animal or plant that is composed of various tissues organized to do certain things in life." A definition that leaves a wide-open door for interpretation.

Even if bone marrow is an organ, I say to myself, *how can this "waiting period" apply to Michael?*

My heart sank a month ago in the Health Sciences Library as I read the medical words that spelled out Michael's illness. Now these legal words in our policy wave a red flag regarding his treatment—and blow me away with disbelief.

Surely words such as these are merely shotgun blasts to scare off transplant shoppers. How can they be so indiscriminately aimed as to include a baby with a sudden onset of leukemia?

An initial denial so inhumane could only be born by something inhuman—likely a computer-generated response to a computer-generated bill.

They will reconsider once they know the facts, I assure myself.

We discover that phoning the insurance company is futile. We become well acquainted with recording machines. We call again and are put on hold. We speak politely and respectfully to the frontline, non-decision-making, complaint screeners, hoping someone in this business will hear the plight of our baby. Will anyone simply listen to the voice of common sense and recognize the plea of parents with a legitimate concern?

In frustration we ask Michael's doctor to write the insurance company. Surely they will listen to the doctor!

Again, we must wait.

While we wait, we receive yet another bill in the mail from the cancer center. The charge for donor typing and blood tests just for our family: $5,000.

We continue to pray Michael's disease doesn't progress, hoping now more than ever that his transplant can be delayed as long as possible. We pray God will heal him without it.

A new and incredible journey begins—a struggle through a jungle of institutional red tape. Hanging over us now is a crushing sum that could fall entirely upon our shoulders. Without batting an eye we would pay it for any one of our children. "But, Lord, how can we pay it?"

The cost of a bone marrow transplant: $200,000.

How could I ever have known this would happen when I moved my family from Omak?

Lord, what have I done?

An Interview With
Dr. Julie Park

Dr. Park, a hematologist/oncologist
at Children's Hospital in Seattle,
was Michael's primary doctor before he went into
the Fred Hutchinson Center.

"I thought it was a tragedy that the insurance company wouldn't pay for something like this. Unfortunately, I'm becoming a bit cynical about how insurance works; I wasn't completely surprised at first that they were denying it. But I thought they might change their mind along the way.

"We knew from previous cases and the medical literature that Michael's disease was something that didn't go away and that it eventually turned into leukemia. Michael had a very big liver and spleen, which probably meant there wasn't a lot of time before that happened.

"The hardest part of Michael's treatment was watching the family go through the period of time before the transplant, telling them their son needed such radical treatment. It was a very hard thing to say—that a transplant was what Michael needed and it could save his life, but it could also kill him."

Chapter Fourteen

HEAVY BURDENS

Y ou load sixteen tons and what do you get? Another day older and deeper in debt."

The words of this once popular song raise a question. Is the daily grind made more burdensome by its load or by its futile end?

It's a question we face when trying to make ends meet. Each month the bills unrelentingly roll in, like waves crashing over our heads. The big one from the Fred Hutchinson Cancer Research Center could certainly drown us in a sea of debt, making our efforts seem meaningless.

What needs to be paid and when? What can wait? Even well-thought-out strategies seem futile if you are climbing the mast of a sinking ship.

When tempted to quit, we're reminded of higher stakes and higher purposes. We recall who is watching, who cares more about what we're becoming than what we're achieving. We know He cares more about our direction than our progress.

For now we must simply look to Him. It's time to roll up our sleeves and unfold our hands, not wring them in discouragement and discontent.

Tears mix with sweat...the stuff fervent prayers are made of.

Considering our present financial position, we first draw a new map to point us in the right direction. We devise a better plan to balance the money equation of income versus outgo.

Our new budget reaffirms our resolve to be givers, to be debt-free, and to be content with having enough to meet basic needs.

The bottom line of our new April plan: restraint. After giving and fixed expenses, $400 in cash is left in an envelope to cover monthly food, gas, clothing, personal care, education, recreation, and miscellaneous expenses. It's a tighter squeeze.

Still, we intend to keep our promise to avoid the bottomless pit of debt. We temporarily park a car because license tabs are due. An inner voice of pride mocks my male soul with taunts of inadequacy. As a husband and father, I am called to be a provider.

Besides teaching full time, I work part time in sales with World Book Educational Products. We originally factored in the extra income to help cover the increased cost of living in the city. Rent for comparable dwelling places jumped from $400 a month in Omak to $875 a month in Seattle. But with Michael's illness there's been little left of me to do extra work.

Kristi is the household engineer, overseeing the departments of health, education, welfare, food, and agriculture (in the form of a garden). She is a stay-at-home mom who homeschools our children. Kristi has always put high value on the preventive measures of good nutrition and home remedies for our family. Now, because of Michael's condition and our insurance situation, she thinks there may be a natural way to build up his immune system and buy time to delay the transplant.

We are thankful over the week of spring break that Michael stays out of the hospital. I take advantage of it by going out and selling encyclopedias. The fruits of my labor increase in April, and another opportunity opens as well.

Omak school officials call and express their interest in hiring me back as a vice principal for next fall. The pay increase and cost of living decrease would provide quick fix answers to our finances but raise bigger questions about Michael's medical care—more questions we must now wrestle with.

Chapter Fifteen

A CRUSHING REPORT

s we enter the month of May, Michael's dropping platelet blood cell counts bother Children's Hospital hematologists. To find out for sure what's going on, they take another bone marrow sample on May 4. And again, we wait.

Over the course of the last few weeks Kristi's attempts to give Michael the vitamins and natural remedies prescribed for him become futile. Michael can't keep the medications down. The doctor has thoroughly compared Michael's blood work and medical records with all the research, but he has determined the best he can do is possibly buy time for Michael.

Sunday, May 10, 1992. Mother's Day. A day specially planned for the very special mother to my children. She is shouldering a tremendous burden and deserves a day to rest, a day to enjoy.

But it is not to be. I wake to the early morning cries of Michael.

I approach his crib and reach my hand out instinctively to his forehead. He feels hot to my touch. Please, not today! My heart sinks as I place the thermometer under his arm and watch it rise to 102.5°. His cries grow more intense. A change of diapers uncovers painfully swollen, red, and infected genitals.

The fever means we must immediately call the hematologist. Not surprisingly, the doctor orders Michael to the emergency room. From there he is again admitted for IV antibiotics and blood cultures.

This time Michael has a severe yeast infection.

Mother's Day for the other moms at church is a day with the entire family, a time to be honored and to celebrate.

For Michael's mom, it is a day of separation, disappointment, and heartache for her baby boy.

Tuesday, May 12. Today we're overjoyed to bring Michael home again; the infection is under control after the two-day hospital stay. The doctor enters the room as I change Michael from his hospital gown, getting him ready for another homecoming.

Dr. Park's initial greeting is characteristically humble and kind. Her gently spoken words soften the impact of the bombshell she drops.

"The laboratory report is in. I'm sorry to say Michael's disease is progressing dangerously fast. He's in transition to acute leukemia and…we need to do the transplant soon. His initial appointment is set for early June. You'll be getting the information in the mail."

Pain. Numbness. "Need to do the transplant soon." The message needs time to sink in. We drive home in silence. A dark, heavy cloud hangs over the evening, even with Michael's homecoming.

I can't help but compare my burden to the one this tiny, innocent one has carried in his brief visit.

Next to his, I've carried nothing.

Chapter Sixteen

PRAYER FOR A BROKEN ONE

S ix o'clock, May 13, 1992. In early morning solitude I lay bare my wounded soul. As I write in my journal, my words form an appeal to the Highest Authority, a prayer addressed to God, my only hope.

My little boy is dying.

I am left with only a meager petition, a heart cry to heaven. I fall before the throne of my good and merciful King, casting before Him the shattered pieces of my soul.

I reach up to God not for a handout nor with a clenched, demanding fist, but with a childlike hand of faith, seeking only the Father's touch. I am satisfied to know only His presence and the power of His love.

The morning stillness moves me with a sense of God's utter compassion. I know I am undeserving and unworthy, and tears flow in communion with Him.

Whatever my lot, I am called simply to be faithful and grateful, to wait for the justice not bound by time, the mercy not limited by circumstances. I am called to wait patiently for the unfolding of His perfect plan.

Enveloped by the crisp, spring morning that is bathed in sunshine, I am warmed in His arms of grace. As I leave for

Kamiakin Junior High, a deep calming comes in a whisper to my soul....

God has everything under control.

Once again, Lord, we commit our precious little boy into Your hands.

Chapter Seventeen

SEEDS OF COMPASSION

Early morning solitude explodes into midmorning frenzy as I arrive at school and prepare for a mass of adolescent humanity: student government elections, assembly campaign speeches. Myriad, lingering things fill my "to do" list with Michael in the hospital.

For a brief moment following the assembly, I visit with our school principal, Steve, a man with a big heart for little people who is anxious about Michael. He invites me into his office so I can tell him about the latest report.

I open up. "We brought Michael home from the hospital yesterday…but the news isn't good."

Steve's probing concern pushes the underlying problems to the surface. Each question reveals another layer of issues…

- Michael's need for an immediate transplant;
- the insurance denial;
- the bills that already burden us;
- my present options: either pursue the higher paying job in Omak or find a comparable one here.

As if listening to another voice, Steve leans forward in his chair. "Jeff," he says, "with your permission I want to propose a fund-raiser to help your family. I'd like to share this with the faculty at this afternoon's staff meeting. Would that be okay?"

At best I had hoped for a shot at an administrative job—not for becoming a charity case. How do you respond to an offer of pure grace? I could not presume or expect this of anyone. Yet I wonder—by what Hand is this man's heart being moved? Surely it mustn't be mine! I realize Steve has been touched by the same spirit of compassion which in the morning stillness moved me.

I'm stunned. "Well, I guess if it's something you really want to do."

I can read the look of a determined mind. Steve's thoughtfulness warms my heart. His offer uplifts me greatly, whatever amount it may bring. Realistically, it can't do much to boost us over such a huge and urgent financial hurdle.

I will miss the afternoon staff meeting. The government is the route I know I must explore, and the Department of Social and Health Services is where I need to go next.

I spend an afternoon at the welfare office, mixed in with a potpourri of needy people. Young mothers with children. Old folks. Men and women without jobs. Decent- and not-so-decent-looking folk. And me—with a $200,000 price tag on my baby.

There's a strange emptiness about being in the welfare office, a strange absence of the goodwill and compassion I felt so recently in Steve's office. Maybe it's the layer upon layer of bureaucracy which undergirds this governmental provision, insulating reluctant, bitter taxpayers from ungrateful, demanding recipients. Layers which disconnect joy from each transaction, devoid of either cheerful giver or tearful receiver.

I come home after filling out paperwork—more hoops to jump through, but no answers. I am referred to a different office, another appointment, with another social worker, for another Monday.

Yet I seek whatever it takes, by any possible means, for a most worthwhile end—the life of my little boy.

An Interview With
Steve Mezich
*Steve is the principal at Kamiakin Junior High School
and Jeff's good friend.*

"On a Wednesday morning Jeff stepped into my office, closed the door, and began to update me on the insurance situation with Michael. Clearly he was drained of all physical and emotional energy. His family was working on its last $500, but Jeff was not looking for anything; he just needed someone to listen.

"Jeff had to leave school to attend to another matter. That afternoon before I started our regular Wednesday staff meeting, I put off the agenda for a moment to tell the staff about Jeff's situation. I felt compelled that we as colleagues do something immediately to help. That was the most emotional faculty meeting I've ever been in.

"The staff started talking about what to do, and when all the dust settled, we had a pretty formal plan. The most heartwarming thing for me was the rallying of Jeff's colleagues. A phenomenal energy poured out of that meeting."

Chapter Eighteen

THE WINDS OF GRACE

I arrive home from the welfare office at five that afternoon and notice a familiar glisten, though not sorrowful, in Kristi's eyes.

"Detra came by while you were gone. Look in the envelope on the table."

After the staff meeting that afternoon, Detra, our vice principal, had made a special visit to bring a bag of toys for the kids. I open her card, read her note of encouragement, and unfold a check tucked inside. Five hundred dollars! An act of generosity that baffles my everyday thinking. It is kindness in the first degree. No, people just don't give away this kind of money.

I pick up the phone. "Detra, this is too much!"

"No, Don and I want you to have it. We want to do what we can to help."

Their little boy suffers from a heart condition. Empathy shatters the pain barrier with love.

The unexpected gift draws from us different tears—quiet, cleansing tears of joy. Hearts broken first by tragedy are broken now by kindness.

Kristi stays home with Michael tonight. I take the kids to

our Wednesday night service at Summit View Community Church. Again we pray.

Thursday morning I arrive at school inspired by Detra's gift and want once more to thank her. I stop by my mailbox to find it filled with more envelopes from the Kamiakin staff—treasures of wishes for Michael's recovery, prayers, loving support, and $350 in cash and checks.

Without doubt, the winds of grace stirred yesterday's staff meeting, lifting the human spirit far above the confines of self.

Grace, like the wind—unseen and uncontained—is known only by the effect outside of itself. Yesterday we had nothing but a prayer; today we see the touch of a powerful God.

An Interview With
Kristi Leeland
Kristi is Michael's mom.

"Detra called from the mall and asked if she could drop by. I said, 'Sure!' I had no idea why she was coming. I think I had only met her once before. So we rushed around the house trying to pick up.

"About ten minutes after the call there was a knock at the door. Standing there was Detra with her two children, each holding shopping bags. I thought it was strange that they were bringing their shopping bags into the house. I thought maybe she was going to show me some wonderful buys they got at the mall!

"But then each of her kids gave our kids presents from the bags. There was a T-ball bat and ball, Barbies—toys for all our kids. Then Detra handed me a card. When I opened it, there was a five-hundred-dollar check folded up inside. Tears started rolling down my cheeks as I read her card. Then Detra came over and hugged me."

An Interview With
Detra Markey

Detra was vice principal at Kamiakin Junior High School and was the first donor in the effort to help the Leeland family.

"Why did I get involved? There were a number of reasons. First of all, I have a son, Brandon, who has medical problems, so I know what that's like as a parent. I wondered, 'What if, in trying to keep Brandon healthy, I faced the obstacle of not being insured when I had done all the things I was supposed to do as an employee?' Jeff is one of the most fair, upright, honest people I know, and to be refused medical attention because of some waiting period felt so unfair to me.

"I also felt the Leelands needed people's help and the only way they were going to get through this was if people just stepped up. I didn't know much about getting the ball rolling with others, but I knew what I could do.

"I discussed with my husband, Don, that I wanted to give Jeff a check to get things moving. Even though it might not mean a lot and it was a long way from being there, I knew that whatever came in would help out. Don said, 'I don't think you should wait until tomorrow at work to give it to him; you should go right over to his house and give it to him now.' So that's what I did."

Chapter Nineteen

UNMISTAKABLY A HERO

Friday, May 15, 3 P.M. School having dismissed a half-hour ago, I sit in my office, looking forward to the relief this weekend will bring. My phone rings.

"Mr. Leeland?"

"Yes."

"I'm Dameon's mom."

"Oh, hi!"

"Dameon came home from school today and asked me to take him to the bank. He wants to withdraw all his savings and give it to you for your little boy."

"You're kidding!" I say, stunned, and then realize she might be upset. "Really, he doesn't have to do that. A card would be just fine."

"No, this is very important to him and it's okay with me. Will you be there in twenty minutes?"

Still in shock, I feebly reply, "I'll be here."

A few minutes later, in walk Dameon and his mom. He approaches me and says, "Mr. Leeland, don't make a big deal out of this, but you're my partner...and if your baby's in trouble, I want to help out."

Then reaching out his hand to mine, Dameon gives me

his life savings—twelve, five-dollar bills all rolled up. Sixty dollars you wouldn't trade for a million.

My heart is deeply touched, and I hug Dameon, a fifth period student from my adaptive physical education class.

"Dameon, you're the kind of guy I'd bring to the trenches with me."

He leaves, walking tall, cloaked with a sense of honor and dignity rarely accorded to such a boy—a proud mother by his side.

I go immediately to Steve's office and tell him the story of Dameon's donation. We agree that with this gift we shall set up a special account at Pacific First Bank.

Later we sit with the administrator, Tina, as she establishes the Michael Leeland Fund. Her eyes tear up when she hears the story behind this opening deposit. Quickly she drafts her own note of appreciation to Dameon.

Dameon. That boy in seventh grade who trudges, with a limp, nearly a mile to school every day. A boy you can't miss, in his black stretch pants, big, white, button-down shirt, and tie. A soft-hearted thirteen-year-old contained in a handicapped body. A boy with a few learning difficulties and a few friends, who faces his own mountains of adversity. Yet this young man is willing to set aside his struggle to lift the burden from my shoulders, willing to sell the farm for my little boy.

One simple act of charity.

As I think about this amazing gesture, I cannot help but wonder: What explains the injustice Dameon endures and the mercy he now expresses; the burden this boy carries and the helping hand he extends; the pain he absorbs and the healing he offers? The explanation comes in a measure of one's character, a different brand of success.

A world impressed with billionaire corporate magnates, political giants of power and influence, personalities of beauty and fame, cannot comprehend the magnitude of such a heart. They all shrink in my eyes before my friend Dameon.

A young boy teaches the teacher
> to see his own difficulties as opportunities;
>> to strengthen his grip on what really matters;
>>> to extend his hand toward others in need.

I thank God for all the Dameons of the world, unsung heroes who inspire us to face the steeper paths of life. They remind us of higher ground and of the Friend who can carry our load.

An Interview With
Dameon Sharkey

Dameon was one of Jeff's students in his adaptive P.E. class.

"I still remember meeting Mr. Leeland. I was your young, lovable kid. I was standing in the background, watching the kids play sports, when this young guy comes over and says, 'You're Dameon Sharkey?' 'Well, yeah,' I say. 'Why do you ask?' 'I'm your teacher,' he says. He makes me get up, and then he says, 'Dameon, I'm going to get you in shape even if it kills you.'

"When you see one P.E. teacher, you've seen 'em all. But this guy put the hook in me. I still hold him in the highest respect. Mr. Leeland helped me a lot. Basically he's my mentor. If it wasn't for him, well…if I ever get married, I'll ask Mr. Leeland to be my best man.

"Anyway, one Friday they were passing out flyers about Michael, and I'm reading this and thinking, 'All right, this guy has helped me through a lot. He pulled me through a lot of rough stuff.' So I sort of ran to the car and said, 'Mom, I've gotta go to the bank. I've gotta wipe out my entire savings account. I've gotta give this to Mr. Leeland.' 'Now, wait a minute, wait a minute, slow down,' she said. 'Just hold it. Why?' 'You know Mr. Leeland?' I asked her. 'Yeah, you told me about him,' she said. 'Well, I want to give him my sixty dollars for his little boy because he needs a bone marrow transplant.' 'Well, okay,' she said, 'but let's call and make sure this is all right.'

"To make a long story short, we go up to his office fifteen minutes later, I hand him sixty dollars, and I say to him, 'The only thing I want from you is a thank you and a smile.'

"Basically, that's what happened. It was the greatest thing I ever did."

Chapter Twenty

FALLING THROUGH
THE CRACKS

O
ur first confirmation letter comes from the Fred Hutchinson Cancer Research Center, also known as "the Hutch." Dated May 11, the letter verifies Michael's referral to the Center for his transplant in June.

A series of outpatient appointments, the "work-up," is scheduled to begin the week of June 8. The readying process will last about two weeks before Michael is admitted for two months to undergo the highly intense bone marrow transplant.

The letter strikes us with another jolt of business world reality. We are informed the center needs a promise to pay from our insurance company or Medicaid by the last week of May—only two weeks away—or else Michael's appointment could be postponed.

It is another, potentially life-threatening delay with our son's disease now in high gear.

Our alternative: to come up with $175,000 deposit! It is a huge amount of money—an impossible sum for the average family to pay in a small window of time.

We intensify our appeal to the institutions in place, "the deep pockets." We earnestly seek the right hoops to jump through, the right people to talk to.

Monday, May 18. Another appointment with the state welfare office, another disappointment. This time…too much income! Teaching salary and encyclopedia sales combine for the month of May to disqualify us from the state and federal program, Medicaid.

This is the irony of eligibility for government help: It doesn't pay to work extra hard or honestly report extra income. We do both simply because it is the right thing to do.

Deep down we still hope the insurance people will come through for Michael. We're even confident they will feel a moral obligation to cover him.

We discover this waiting period on transplants—this narrow, deathly deep crack in health care benefits—was never intended to prevent a baby like Michael from getting help. It was designed as a deterrent for the long-term patient who goes shopping for coverage for this expensive treatment. Nevertheless, this has become the hole we've unwittingly fallen into.

We wait again as the center's financial counselor works with us, formally appealing to the insurance company and requesting coverage for Michael's urgent need.

They will reconsider, I must believe.

What policeman would not usher a desperate father through a yellow light like this—or even a red one!—to get his dying baby urgent medical care?

But to our shock we receive days later another written denial: "The patient is *not* eligible for benefits. This service is subject to the contract waiting period of twelve months for organ transplants. Mr. Leeland's policy became effective 10-1-91."

Don't they understand? Michael may not live until October!

According to the company, "A contract is a contract."

According to me, this exclusion seems unconscionable in Michael's situation. Apparently, to this particular company, it isn't.

I fear that in this business, as in so many other places in modern society, the small voice of conscience is being drowned out completely by the constant, overpowering scream of dollars and cents and litigation. It is a repulsive language we have so far refused to learn.

Overwhelmed now by the price tag on Michael's life and facing a ransom we cannot pay, the urgency of his need forces us as parents to choose one of two emotional pathways. One, a way of demands, anger, anxiety, fear. The other, a way of trust, to be at peace in the face of disappointment, to do what's loving, true, and good despite the circumstances, to have hope for a better tomorrow.

We choose the path of grace instead of vengeance.

If God is the One who keeps an inventory of hair on each human head, the One who cares even for the sparrow that falls to the ground, then surely He will embrace our little boy as the apple of His eye. Our faith will not be in vain. His compassion will not fail.

Even now as our baby hangs over the edge of this deep hole, dangling only by the thread of human compassion, our peace rests in the everlasting arms of God...our ultimate insurance.

An Interview With
Ralph Jones
Ralph is Kristi's father; Michael's grandfather.
He formerly served at PEMCO—*an insurance company*
whose employees raised funds for Michael.

"The insurance company has a tough job of staying with a contract but trying to be human within that contract as much as it can.

"I felt helpless—that's a lot of money to raise real quick. I didn't have the money and no one else did, either.

"So many of the people at Pemco latched onto our family's problem almost as if it were their own. It was amazing. It became a very personal thing to all of them. The way everyone responded was an answer to prayer."

Chapter Twenty-one

KIDS TO THE RESCUE

Teenagers—preadults in limbo-land—hang around for something important to do. They are a breed often looked down upon by the workaday adult world which can't find anything important for them to do.

I'm a teacher, so kids are my business. Maybe they have to matter to me. But I'm glad they do because they make an incredible difference. They've added much more to my life than I could ever hope to give them.

And, believe it or not, there are a lot of teachers who feel the same way. I'm thinking of one in particular: Joe Kennedy, Kamiakin's humanities teacher. Joe is committed to empowering students, to breaking down traditional classroom walls, to building a heart for learning within. Joe establishes a reason for excellence through serving real needs. He finds important things for kids to do.

Joe Kennedy turns our family's crisis into his classroom's curriculum, an education born of inspiration, dedication, preparation, cooperation, and 110 percent perspiration.

Michael becomes a real-life story problem in the hands of these hyperactive, high-spirited, limit-challenging, junior high kids. They race to Michael's rescue. Untainted by the

logical skepticism of the more "mature" that breeds "paraly-
sis of analysis," these idealistic adolescents set the pace with
an unsophisticated passion to save our baby's life. These
remarkable kids issue a challenge to boycott a multimillion-
dollar insurance company. They are kids who make plans:

walkathon,

  raffle,

    donation boxes,

      letters to Ross Perot and Bill Gates, pleading for
      financial help,

        petitions,

          media contacts, requesting news coverage.

These kids make personal sacrifices. The ninth grade
class donates the proceeds from its dance to Michael, money
that would have gone toward an end-of-the-year party. Mary,
an eighth grade student, cashes in her three hundred dollars
in savings bonds. Kristen, a ninth grader, stuffs a donation
box with a hundred dollars at the dance. Jon, another ninth
grader, knocks on doors in his neighborhood, bringing in
checks and cash.

The whole climate of Kamiakin Junior High is changed by
compassion. Students, faculty, staff, and administration are united,
not by a fund-raiser, but by a mission of mercy.

We are awestruck by this outpouring of love, inspiration,
and energy from the kids as they rip the baton from teachers'
hands in a race for Michael's life.

Yes, kids, you can show the business world that one of
your own really does matter. You can make a difference.

You're already champions in my heart.

An Interview With
Joe Kennedy

Joe teaches an advanced humanities class at Kamiakin Junior High and was the teacher who challenged the school's students to see what they could do to help Michael.

"We found out about Michael through Steve Mezich at a faculty meeting. He came in and told the faculty members that Jeff had left for the day and that his son was in a predicament. The meeting was called for another reason, but the agenda pretty much became Michael after that. There was a lot of talking and people asking what they could do.

"I was just one of many teachers who discussed it with their kids afterwards. I had a dedicated class, a class that wanted to go out and make a difference. The kids took the challenge and jumped at the opportunity to do something. It was really fun to see them go for the gusto.

"Kids began to say, 'Let's do this, let's do that.' It was a domino effect. One kid said, 'Let's do a walkathon.' Another responded, 'Oh, walkathons don't make that much money.' The first kid replied, 'Hey, listen, every dime will help.' And the other kid said, 'Yeah, you're right. That was pretty stupid to say.' And so they did the walkathon."

Chapter Twenty-two

WINDOWS TO OUR WORLD

A full-color, five-by-eight-inch picture of Michael and Kristi appears next to the bold, front page headlines: "BOY'S LIFE HANGS ON BY THREAD."

The story is a result of Kamiakin students appealing to the media. I can't believe it made the front page!

Michael sits on his mother's lap, the picture of innocence with feathery blond hair and big blue eyes staring directly into the camera. The candid, distantly forlorn look on Kristi's face tells a story that will eventually grip the emotions of many.

The article on Thursday, May 21, in the *Journal American* opens with, "God is greater than any problem I have." "A sentiment," it says, "the Leelands are relying heavily on." The quote comes from a card that stands over our kitchen sink. We are surprised, unaware the reporter had even noticed it. The closing paragraph describes Dameon's gift.

The evening before, the Seattle *Times* had run a similar article headlined, "Family Scrambles to Pay for Transplant."

These articles present Michael's story in a simple, straightforward way but add the sense of panic from which our faith has shielded us. Each graciously advertises the

Michael Leeland Fund, an account set up at the corner bank from the small, but powerful, seed of Dameon's sixty-dollar gift.

Preoccupation with Michael's immediate health drains our energy and passion for fund-raising. Even so, our friends—and now strangers—willingly give, unwilling to wait in line behind a system that drags its feet.

Friday, May 22. The groundswell of love and generosity overflows from Kamiakin and spills over into the community. The day after the *Journal* article releases, a man walks into the bank with a check for ten thousand dollars. A second grade girl walks into the school office and hands over a sack full of pennies—the contents of her piggy bank—and a letter for Baby Michael.

In our hearts, both gifts are immeasurable!

One week after Dameon's gift of sixty dollars, Michael's account grows to sixteen thousand dollars!

With eyes of faith now lifted up, we find encouragement to press on. We know the worst may yet confront us, so we will cling to the hand of our loving Father. Better to follow Him through the darkness than to cower alone in self-protection!

"Whatever happens, God, we again leave it all in Your hands. We want to follow Your way." Even a king's heart is like a stream of water in the palm of His hand. Surely He can change the direction of an insurance executive's heart, if He so wills!

May 24. A sunny, Sunday afternoon picnic with Grandpa and Grandma, aunts and uncles, cousins—and Channel 7 television news.

Television! Unbelievable! A producer from the Seattle

CBS affiliate station, KIRO, had called early this morning before church to arrange a story about Michael.

Of course we are not expecting many people to be inside watching the Sunday evening news on a beautiful Memorial weekend. Nevertheless, we're thankful for the coverage.

We eat, laugh, and play at Edmonds Park, having been instructed to ignore the camera in our midst—unnaturally trying to look natural.

TV news: two hours of taping for a two-minute story!

At six that evening we anxiously huddle in front of the television to view our lives, seeing our situation from the outside looking in. Could this really be our story, airing now to the whole Northwest?

We see shots of Michael in his stroller, bouncing on his daddy's legs, playful and smiling. We notice his bruised forehead, a telltale sign of the fatal bone marrow disease. The announcer explains our boy is at the mercy of an insurance company, a powerful financial machine, which even now is unthinkably denying his life-saving transplant.

The newscast closes with an appeal to send donations to the Michael Leeland Fund, Pacific First Bank, Kingsgate Branch.

Again, these new advocates for Michael's cause spontaneously step forward.

Again, to whom shall we attribute this amazing grace?

Neither Kristi nor I have asked anyone for money, except for the insurance company, the state, and our Lord.

It is now becoming clearer to us that as the man-made institutions we feverishly cling to fail us, God will provide in His own perfect time and in His own perfect way. He is faithfully about His business of warming the hearts of those whom He would have willingly share in Michael's healing.

We are emptied, only to be filled with more faith in our God to work His means to His perfect end to our dilemma. Somehow, He brings intangible peace in the midst of tangible uncertainty.

If the funds are not there by the deadline, we will trust it is for Michael's best.

Maybe God has a better plan.

An Interview With
Wendy Jones
Wendy is Michael's aunt.

"We got calls, of course, not only from our friends in this area but from friends and relatives in Alaska, in Pennsylvania. 'How can we help?' people wanted to know. Friends of friends of friends came out of the woodwork.

"A thrift shop contacted my cousin and sent a check to Michael's fund. I mean, a thrift shop—they're not rich. The check was for two hundred dollars.

"Where my mom worked, they passed the hat and raised about two thousand dollars. These are not wealthy people, but I think everybody had the sense that what the insurance company had done wasn't fair and that the Leelands needed help.

"We had a one-day garage sale with items donated by a lot of people. We sold hot dogs and did a lot of other stuff and took in about nine hundred dollars that day.

"Many people were concerned and involved. Everybody had the same sense: 'We're going to fight the big corporation here. This is not right.'

"I never felt a sense of hopelessness. It wasn't a bunch of people running around, wringing their hands; it was methodical and careful. It wasn't that we were cocky or over-confident; it simply wasn't in our hands. We could try to get the funding by getting the word out, but the final call was not ours. We knew that."

Chapter Twenty-three

A TIDAL WAVE
OF COMPASSION

Tuesday night, May 26. This is one time I am grateful for continuous busy signals. We phone the number spread across our TV screen at the end of Channel 4's eleven o'clock news.

Yesterday, Memorial Day, our friend Craig Ronning called to tell us he had contacted the Seattle ABC affiliate station, KOMO, and asked if they would do a story on Michael. The producer, having seen the article in the newspaper last week, hesitated at first. It might be old news by now. But then he agreed, thinking perhaps it would fill the late night news slot.

At 9:30 this morning Kristi, Amy, Michael, and I sat on our living room couch in front of the camera for our second unexpected TV interview in two days. Elisa Jaffe, the reporter, asked the questions we have now become familiar with.

We showed her the two documents, letters which spell out our predicament: one from the cancer center, the other from our insurance company. Both press us between the hard lines of an urgent financial deadline and a denial of coverage.

As Elisa heard our testimony and saw our baby Michael, tears welled up in her eyes. "I've never cried in an interview!" she confessed. A deep nerve was touched, and she put her heart into the story.

"We're going to try to get this on the 6:30 news," she declared.

But first they stopped downtown to talk with the insurance company.

I missed the dinnertime newscast that evening, arriving home after a late meeting. I anxiously anticipated word if Michael's story was aired.

As I walked in, Jaclyn met me at the door, unusually bothered. "Dad, you should have seen it! That insurance company said they would let Michael die!"

At the end of the clip, the anchorwoman, Kathi, with misty eyes simply read the station phone number for any viewers wanting to help out.

I hoped for an eleven o'clock rerun to see for myself. We waited and excitedly watched later that evening as the news came on.

"The response has been incredible for a little Bothell boy," Kathi began. Again the station ran Elisa's heartfelt version of Michael's dilemma, as well as the insurance company's cold response. Once more the station phone number flashed on the screen as the story ended.

After twenty minutes of dialing, it is close to midnight before my call finally gets through. "Hi, I'm Michael's dad, Jeff Leeland. I just wanted to thank you for the story."

"Oh, let me transfer you to Kathi."

The anchorperson immediately comes on. "We've never seen anything like this before!" she declares. In amazement she describes the unprecedented response to the story. The station phone lines have been flooded since the 6:30 news. By nine o'clock an elderly woman named Jeanne has called to report she has already set up phone chains for prayer and support in thirteen towns and cities across Southwest Washington!

A tidal wave jolts the television air waves, stirring the waters of many souls, sweeping us away in a flood of compassion.

We are weary, but ecstatic. Things are out of our hands, but in other hands.

Tonight we go to bed with unbelievable hope.

An Interview With
Jeanne Robb
*Jeanne is a grandmother living in the
Washington community of Shelton.
Even though she had never met Michael or the Leeland family,
Jeanne began phone chains that stretched across the state.*

"We had just finished dinner on a Tuesday night as the 6:30 news came on Channel 4. I always watch *Oprah Winfrey*, but when I went to do the dishes, my husband took the clicker and switched channels. So I was doing dishes and listening to the news. When I heard about this little boy, I went over to the counter and watched it.

"I thought back to when my son's little boy had died and my daughter's little girl had died and there wasn't anybody who could do anything! All of a sudden it came to me that I was able to do something to help Michael live. From out of the blue I just knew he was going to make it and that I could help make it happen!

"I called KOMO, Channel 4, and asked for the name and address of the bank where you could send money because they had said it too fast on the news. As soon as I got it, I began to call the people on our church's prayer chain, and I asked if they would do three things. Pray for Michael—that was first. The second was to give as much as they thought they could afford to help Michael live. And the third thing was to call friends, neighbors, relatives—only people they knew so it wouldn't be uncomfortable—and ask each one of them to do the same thing to keep it going, like a chain letter.

"I called sixty people, and I asked each of them to call at least five others but more if possible. You can imagine how many hundreds of people were involved before the evening was over!

"Then I thought, 'All churches have prayer chains.' So I opened the phone book and started going down the list of the churches in Shelton. And I asked each of them to contact the people on their prayer chains and do the same thing. Most of them had forty or fifty people on their prayer chains so that involved hundreds more people.

"Next I called churches in Belfair and people I know in fifteen other towns and asked them to contact their churches' prayer chains. I went as far east as Richland, as far south as Portland, as far north as Port Angeles, and as far west as Aberdeen—all the different towns around here where I know people. So there were all those churches calling their prayer chains and then all their friends, neighbors, and relatives.

"I called for eighteen and a half hours! You can imagine how many people I talked to! A couple of days later a radio station called me and did a live telephone interview. When they asked what people should do to help, I explained, 'Call your churches' prayer chains. Call your friends, your neighbors, your relatives, and tell them about this little boy. Pray for him and send whatever you can,' and I gave the address of the bank. I don't know how many people were reached by the radio station; they called twice.

"I couldn't do a thing to help my grandson or my granddaughter. In the blink of an eye both of them were gone. But I knew I could help this little boy. I felt like I was his grandmother. I knew what to tell these people, and they couldn't do enough to help me; it was like magic almost. At the time I did this I was quite sick with pneumonia and all kinds of complications, but it got my mind totally off of how I felt, and it made my spirits fly!"

Chapter Twenty-four

THE FLOODGATES
OF HEAVEN

I wake up the next morning, Wednesday, May 27, to the insistent ringing of the phone.

"Mr. Leeland?"

"Yes."

"This is KOMO TV news. We'd like to come to Kamiakin today to cover everything the students are doing for Michael. Michael will be the feature story in the evening newscast."

We are now riding the wave of public interest.

Later that morning Kamiakin Junior High buzzes with activity. Volunteer students collect money from donation boxes in all the classrooms and sell raffle tickets at lunchtime for the donated car, helicopter ride, and cord of firewood. They also collect pledge sheets for the walkathon scheduled for tomorrow afternoon.

No fewer than three separate news teams converge on us today. The five o'clock evening news opens with live coverage from the track meet after school. They air earlier interviews with students involved in fund-raising efforts, showcasing the inspiring sacrifices of kids.

The evening news at half past six covers more of the

story. The eleven o'clock news team follows us to church that night and broadcasts prayers and songs of thanks. Kristi is asked, "How do you feel about all this?"

"This is incredible," she says, overwhelmed. "We want to thank everyone!"

But most of all we want to give credit where credit is ultimately due. That is why we are here tonight, like other Wednesday evenings, in church.

The station is deluged now with phone calls from people asking how they might help. Channel 4 becomes a barometer of growing public interest in the inspirational efforts of the kids and the growing fund for Michael.

Like an official scorekeeper in a race against time, KOMO keeps the dollar amounts in front of viewers with regular "Michael updates" on the news. Each update closes with our boy's face in the corner of the screen, accompanied by the bank address for the Michael Leeland Fund.

The floodgates of heaven begin opening and showering their abundance down upon us. Letters, letters, and more letters pour down. Many contain just checks. Some have no return address.

Hundreds and hundreds of checks pour in. Boxes of letters assuring us of the prayers of unknown brothers and sisters stream in. Others are letters of outrage toward a system that would let a baby die. Still others express empathy and support.

Moms and dads all over the Northwest share our brokenness and put themselves in our shoes. They describe how they held their little ones tight as they tearfully watched the news.

All are letters of comfort. Many pour out their hearts,

sharing their own private victories and losses.

On one day, Thursday, May 28, nine thousand dollars pour in. The Michael Leeland Fund compounds daily, growing to thirty-three thousand dollars! Even at this point, the spirit of generosity is much more inspiring than the figures.

The next day we are stunned by reports from the bank. Hundreds upon hundreds of unknown, faceless strangers send in—on one day—nearly thirty thousand dollars for our son!

How can this be? The Michael Leeland Fund on Friday, May 29, stands at sixty-two thousand dollars!

The whole complex of events spotlights the enigma of human nature. In April, just one month earlier, we sat in front of the same television news and saw a totally different image of humanity. Atrocities in Los Angeles. Riots. Looting. Burning. Beating. Street injustice without a hint of rationality or sense. We were shocked and sickened at man's brutal inhumanity to his fellow man.

Now, that dark backdrop of evil contrasts sharply with the Artist's divine brush strokes of goodness and light as He moves the hearts of those willing to be His instruments of mercy. He masterfully paints His beautiful picture of love and grace indelibly on our souls.

How can we ever again look at our fellow man with the same skeptical eyes? Those who once seemed to be cold, uncaring, distant, Seattle city dwellers now come alive as warm, compassionate neighbors uniting in love for our little boy.

"Lord, who truly has changed—them or me?"

An Interview With
Tina Kelley

*Tina is the administrator at the Bothell branch of
Washington Mutual Bank,
formerly Pacific First, where
the Michael Leeland Fund was established.*

"I first got involved with Michael's story when Jeff and Steve, the principal from Kamiakin, came down with Dameon's sixty dollars and decided to open an account for Michael. Slowly the word got out—the newspapers picked it up, and then the word spread. We were getting tons of mail a day. We received some heartbreaking, wonderful letters. We did the bookkeeping for it and had a thermometer chart of the goal and where we were in reaching it.

"And we got phone calls like crazy—it was so exciting. The very first call was from an elderly gentleman who said, 'Those darn business people! Can't they give a little boy a break? I'm going to take my ax and go chop down their building!' About three days later we got a donation apparently from the same gentleman. His note said, 'I still might take an ax to that building. Those people aren't very fair!' Other letters said things like, 'We were in the same situation. My heart goes out to you.' All the letters said, 'We can't let that little lad down.'

"Contributions varied from a dollar to ten thousand dollars. Letters came from as far away as Florida and Arkansas. They never said how they heard—maybe they were vacationing here or read an article in the paper. It was pretty exciting.

"Everything happened in four short weeks. My desk was half-full of mail. Kamiakin was sending down two or three kids to help us open all the mail so we could get it deposited.

"We were just waiting for the day when Michael was going to have that transplant. Our prayers were with them. All of us in the branch were involved—a big family group effort with the school. It was just like Michael was everybody's boy."

An Interview With
Joe Kennedy

Joe taught the advanced humanities class at Kamiakin Junior High and was the teacher who challenged the school's students to see what they could do to help Michael.

"The kids were on TV, walking down the road with big signs for Michael. I think that really showed the community something, because they walked through the community. People were motivated that way. The kids were the impetus that got a lot of things going.

"All you had to do was see the newscasts. The focus wasn't that money was coming in; the focus was that the kids had rallied to pull everything together.

"I remember that year because the kids asked me to speak at the end-of-the-year dinner. I talked about the words they had taken out of their vocabulary that year: 'can't do' and 'impossible.' Those were gone. The kids proved they can do anything they want and that nothing's impossible. They were really, really excited about helping another kid they didn't even know."

An Interview With
Denise Toal

*Denise was a student at Kamiakin
who helped raise money for Michael
through a walkathon.
She subsequently spent time in Children's
Hospital herself to have a tumor removed from her kidney.*

"Michael's sickness brought a lot of people together. They were really worried about Mr. Leeland and his little boy. Some of the people were like Dameon, who gave up his savings for Michael. And some people gave a lot of their money and didn't even think about saving any for themselves. They just wanted to give it all to Michael.

"In hematology/oncology you're with a lot of kids like yourself who have lost their hair. So you think, 'Oh they're going through what I'm going through. Am I luckier than they are? Am I going to make it?' Some of them become your friends, and you wonder what's going to happen with them. Together you learn how to live, and you share your stories. And everybody prays to God because they're all so worried and scared.

"I think it's made me a lot stronger. I went to church and prayed before, but going through this made me realize how much I needed the Lord. It's made our family become closer. And you get to know a lot of the people around you and at your church."

Michael's Story

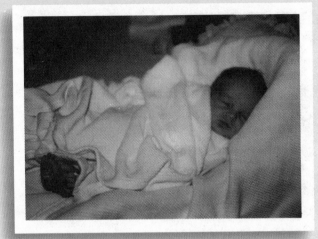

Michael Jeffrey Leeland is born August 19, 1991.

As Jeff moves to
Seattle to start his new
teaching job, the
family is left behind—
Amy, Kristi, Jaclyn,
Kevin, and Michael.

Michael's Story

In between hospital stays, six-month-old Michael is the picture of a happy baby boy.

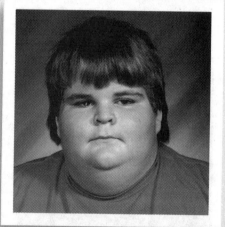

Dameon, a seventh grade boy, donates his entire savings account to Michael, and with his $60 the Michael Leeland Fund is established.

Tina Kelley, the Pacific First Bank administrator, stands in front of the poster which charts the donations that miraculously come pouring into the bank.

Kristi gives Michael his daily "scrub in the tub" to keep his body sterile. An enlarged liver and spleen from the leukemia give his stomach a swollen appearance.

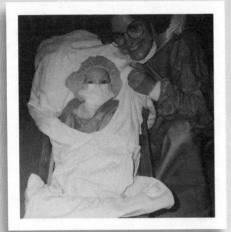

Pam, one of Michael's nurses, has him sterilely bundled for a wagon ride to the hospital basement to undergo another bout of radiation.

The LAF curtain, a sterile barrier to protect Michael from infection, also separates him from skin-to-skin contact for fifty days.

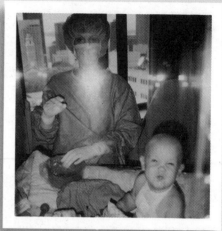

Michael remains playful even with the Hickman line inserted in his chest, which is wrapped to prevent him from pulling the tube out.

August 19, 1992. Michael's first birthday is celebrated in isolation as he admires his cake from inside his protective environment.

Michael's Story

December, 1992. Little by little as Michael's new marrow begins protecting him, he can go out in public.

At two and a half years old Michael's growth pattern is normal. Since earlier tests indicated that Michael was producing no growth hormone, the specialist says, "I have no explanation!"

Michael's Story

Hidden inside Amy's bones were the marrow cells which became Michael's hope for life——a rare match that cemented a bond for life.

Three candles on a birthday cake! Michael's third birthday celebrates the greatest gift of all——life itself.

Chapter Twenty-five

FROM TRAGEDY
TO TRIUMPH

F riday afternoon, May 29. We wrap up a frenzied week
of activity at school. Yesterday, a six-mile walkathon for
Michael, featuring one hundred banner-waving, chant-
ing, junior high kids. Today, the raffle for a car and other
donated prizes. The end of an unbelievable week!

On the downside, the month of May ends without our
having verification of insurance coverage or the required
$175,000 deposit. Michael's first appointment will be
pushed back to the end of June.

The month also ends with Michael's health seriously
deteriorating. Our son is hospitalized over the weekend with
another infection and high fever. A dangerously low platelet
count is close to shutting down his systems completely; it
stands at 5,000 when it should be 200,000.

We can see more bruises just from normal crawling.
Petechia—tiny reddish dots just under the surface of
Michael's soft skin as blood seeps from his capillaries—
shows when he cries hard.

Michael is in need of transfusions, an unmistakable sign
of acute leukemia. How much longer can he wait? The

deadly, two-edged sword is falling as Michael's leukemia progresses even as infections increase. His chances are sliced with each delay, further diminishing hope of treatment.

We look upon this little one, so precious, as he clings to the edge of life. We grasp his tiny hand helplessly and feel him slipping through our fingers.

Our baby. Leukemia.

June brings more bittersweet experiences. Michael is hospitalized thirteen out of the first fourteen days of the month. Yet we are recipients of amazing blessings as well.

Like living in a dream world, we are crushed one moment by a nightmarish dilemma, while the next moment a beautiful love story restores our faith and hope. Each day is a mixture of deep pain and incredible love.

The newscasts follow Michael to the hospital where we watch, astonished, as the fund grows in leaps and bounds despite our distance and lack of involvement.

Monday, June 1. The bank is being swamped with deposits and calls to help. Moms from school volunteer to open mail. Another $30,000 pours in over the weekend with the biggest single donation being $500.

The Michael Leeland Fund grows to $91,000 total! How can we explain this? What compels such energy and passion?

Tuesday, June 2. The total reaches $111,000. Another $20,000 deposited in one day!

I watched a movie once where a young mother was paddling a canoe around a lake, her baby girl cradled inside. Suddenly, unexpected waves hit the boat and capsized it! Both mother and baby went under. The mother quickly surfaced, panicked and screaming, but her baby was still helplessly submerged.

I remember in that one terrifying instant my breath being taken away. The thought of this baby girl drowning caused every muscle in my body to tense. I wanted to dive through the TV screen to save the helpless child. Gallantly, a man jumped in and swam out from the shore. The seconds seemed like hours as he dove under. Moments later, he broke the surface...holding the gasping baby. Alive! Thank God! In the arms of a hero.

A television drama versus a real-life drama. Unknown people are diving in to save our baby, jumping in from every shore for Michael. Friends, family, fellow church members, former classmates, former students, former teammates, former coaches, strangers, out-of-the-woodwork outsiders, completely unknown friends.

More school kids jump in. Cascade High School students raise $4,500 in one week with a taco eating contest and a dunk tank.

My former students at Omak High School start their own fund for Michael. One elementary classroom gives its pizza money to Michael instead of having its class party.

Big people are making a difference—getting donations, holding raffles, writing letters, holding garage sales to save our baby boy.

Little people are making a difference—breaking their piggy banks, breaking our hearts.

Heroes all.

Wednesday, June 3: $124,000!

Mail. Tons of mail. This letter, dated May 28, from a man named Tom, is one we especially cherish:

Dear Leeland Family, I am $35,000 in debt and have no job, and when I hear about stories like this, I realize how small my problems are. I have my health, and I hope $10 will help. It's what I'm able to do. God bless Michael. He has my prayers.

The Toms of this world—the weak, the innocent—they hold the power to move us most deeply, to inspire us far more by their attitude than the fortunate and powerful do by their attainments.

Inspiration is born not in the size of the spoil but in the size of the battle.

Friday, June 5. The total climbs to $143,000. Businesses dive in to help. Many offices and restaurants take collections. QFC, a Seattle-based grocery chain where Michael's Uncle Greg works, buys full-page newspaper ads describing Michael's plight. Donation canisters appear at every checkout stand in all thirty-six stores throughout King County.

Monday, June 8. The Michael Leeland Fund reaches $160,000.

Like being in the eye of a hurricane, I find myself in quiet awe. We watch from the inside of a hospital room as the awesome power of love strikes full fury against impossible odds. In stillness we wait by our son, standing firmly upon our Rock.

Tuesday, June 9. The new total reaches $185,000! The TV news pronounces the victory for Michael. Kamiakin Junior High kids break the surface, holding a drowning child—the baby Michael—in their arms, a whole community at their side.

Our baby will get a second chance!

A scant four weeks after Dameon's gift of $60 opened the floodgates the Michael Leeland Fund now totals over $220,000.

Tragedy has turned into triumph.

An Interview With
Tom and Molly Flick
*Tom is a former University of Washington
football teammate of Jeff's.
He and his wife, Molly, are friends of the Leelands.*

"When I looked in the paper and saw the story about Michael, my heart just dropped," Molly recalls. "I couldn't believe it. I was amazed that this could happen so fast.

"I'm the type of person who thinks you can do something if you just get the word out. And I felt a real urgency. I took several newspaper articles that featured Michael's story and made tons of copies. Then I wrote a handwritten note saying, 'My friend, Jeff Leeland, needs your help. Please, won't you do anything you can?' I've always been good about keeping addresses, so I just went through our mailing list. We've come to know a lot of different people, and I figured with the Husky people and Christian friends that we knew, people would respond with an open heart."

"There's a pretty tight network of Husky players," Tom adds. "Jeff and I come from the era when it was all new to win a bowl game. Now it's expected, but that was the beginning of Coach James's Husky football period. We were and still are a real close group."

But Molly was not done. "Then I went to a toddler group for my son and told my girlfriend Lisa about it," she explains. "I said, 'We've got to do something about this.' We made calls and had copy machines going and were faxing people all over the place. We felt an urgency to get the word out and believed that as soon as it was out, people would respond.

"Even my three-year-old son was really involved and helped me stuff envelopes. When they would show the story on TV, he'd say, 'We're saving Michael—there he is!' And we'd pray for baby Michael. Every time we saw Michael in the paper, he knew who it was immediately without anyone pointing it out. He would say, 'There's baby Michael. He's getting better.'"

"When QFC put canisters at every checkout counter and put things on the bags, I had a sense that the message had gone out," says Tom. "It made you cry. You knew it was going to be accomplished, that it was just a matter of time—especially when they did counts on the radio each week to report how much those stores had pulled in."

"It made you feel good that people who didn't even know the Leelands would respond as they did," adds Molly. "I'd get choked up whenever I'd go to the checkout. And I'd tell people, 'We know Jeff and we're going to get the money. And I'm so thankful that you're helping.' The word got out so well and the community responded. People felt good about helping. It was amazing; you could really sense a community.

"It was a small-town feeling because of the people's coming together. It was really unusual. Seattle's a big town and to have that feeling just made you feel good, like everyone was pulling for Michael."

The Community Responds

Scores of independent, unrelated fund-raising drives were undertaken all over the Seattle area in an effort to get Michael the money he needed for his transplant.

At Providence Hospital in Seattle a young woman set up a table for donations, graced with Michael's picture, and raised a thousand dollars. "One lady came up on a bus from Mississippi," she says. "She had three kids with her, she was a single mom, and she was homeless. She also was a battered mother whose uncle had helped her buy the bus ticket up to Seattle. But she came by the table, told me her story, and put money in the container."

The Phi Delta Theta house, Jeff's college fraternity, joined the cause by sponsoring an all-day battle of the bands for Michael, raising about two thousand dollars. A fraternity brother whom Jeff had not seen for fourteen years sent a check for five thousand dollars to the bank.

Hair stylists in the region had a haircutting day in which they donated five dollars to the Michael Leeland Fund for every haircut they gave.

Employees of the insurance company denying Michael coverage reached out to him individually, including a personal check for fifty dollars that came from an administrator. Other insurance companies' employees joined in as well. Pemco workers united to contribute a large sum.

A state agency known as "peaches" (PCHS, a children's health division) sent a letter and check from their office. Again, they gave not as a state agency but as individual people who cared.

A twenty-five-dollar check was issued from the state penitentiary, a donation for Michael from an inmate.

Relatives, acquaintances, close friends, and long lost friends drew near to offer tremendous support financially, practically, and spiritually. Some donated thousands of dollars. Money was generated by everything from garage sales to the sale of a piece of property. Children sent personal cards and allowances.

Some Microsoft employees with connections to Kamiakin Junior High challenged their company to match funds donated by employees. With help from the Fred Hutchinson Cancer Research Center, Microsoft opened the door for corporate donations by contributing to the Patient Care Fund, another financial safety net for Michael and potentially for future patients. Eventually "the Hutch" named this campaign the Research Care Fund, a fund to help cover costs of promising treatments for transplant patients, yet treatments still deemed experimental by insurance companies.

Craig Ronning needed to get ten thousand tickets printed for a raffle scheduled to take place at a sports card show the next morning. When he went to buy blank tickets and told the store owner they were for Michael, he received all ten thousand free. Next he went to a print shop to have information about the raffle printed on the tickets. The shop owner put all other jobs on hold, and then she, another employee, and Craig printed and loaded tickets in boxes for the better part of a day—a job worth hundreds of dollars. When Craig tried to pay, she said, "I don't know why I'm doing this, but I won't accept your money." Craig said later, "It seemed as if every door we tried to open in order to raise funds for Michael was unlocked."

An Interview With
Steve Mezich

Steve was the principal at Kamiakin Junior High School
and is Jeff's good friend.

"The people at the bank called us with a note of panic in their voices. They had been inundated with mail for Michael. When I went down there and saw our kids and parents sitting on the floor, helping to sort and count the money, it took a fair amount of composure to hold myself together.

"We sent people down to the bank for two weeks. As I sat there with people I didn't even know—parents of Kamiakin students—I felt overwhelmed by the generosity and love and prayers of people in the community. Someone would stop and say, 'I've got to read this one to you!' There were touching letters and poems and, of course, checks. It made me genuinely love and appreciate the people in our community.

"I don't think anyone will ever know what it did for our school and community. It made the kids realize what they could do. And the kids really did lead the way."

Chapter Twenty-six

SAYING THANK YOU

S itting at my desk one evening, I reflect on the giving that has enveloped us. How could we ever repay so much love given by so many?

Looking to my left, out the window, the reflection of a child's small handprint reaches from the glass and grips my soul.

How our lives are touched by children! Their love, devotion, and simple innocence. Their genuineness. So unstained by the world, so fresh from above...approaching pure grace.

Within moments, words rise into my awareness.

> Tiny hands leave a deep impression—a
> handprint on my heart....
>   Little handprints on the window,
>   Handprints on the wall,
> Five small fingers each remind us
>   Of rules to live by, one and all.
>   First, remember God your Father;
>   In childlike faith upon Him lean;
> Guard your innocence as treasure;
>   Strive to keep your conscience clean.

Don't forget we're all still growing;
We all will stumble as we learn;
Love your sisters and your brothers;
Give to those who can't return.
Last, take time to keep life simple;
Balance work with fun and play;
And when you see this little handprint,
Remember the little one as you pray.

Lessons from children, fundamental values. Approaching simplicity once again after going full circle around a complicated world. These are lessons of childlike faith in God, of purity, growth, love, enjoying life.

The next day we put Michael's hand on an ink pad and impress it beside the poem with "Michael says" just above and "Thank you" just below. This is it, Michael's personally autographed thank-you card with all our signatures.

Then I go out to the copy center and make hundreds of thank-you cards. Melissa, the student body president at Kamiakin, and her friends volunteer to address the cards by hand in her living room night after night, using the return addresses from all the letters and checks.

Jaclyn, Amy, Kevin, and friends sit at our dining room table day after day, licking and sticking stamps.

Hundreds of cards lead to thousands. In all, nearly four thousand are sent out. We read, save, and cherish the hundreds and hundreds of cards and letters that accompanied the gifts.

They are all treasures, legacies of love, constant reminders that we're never alone, that everyone has something to give, that everyone matters. We never want these new friends to forget how much they mean to our family, to Michael. Especially the ones most overlooked, the ones most often forgotten, like the eighty-year-old man who washes dishes for a living and could send Michael only one dollar.

Yes, dear sir, you matter. You made a difference. There will always be a place for you in our hearts.

An Interview With
Melissa Jackson
*Melissa was a ninth grader at Kamiakin Junior High
School and was serving as president of the student body when
Michael's dilemma became known.*

"Mr. Kennedy walked into our humanities class one day and told us about Michael. Everybody was shocked and hurt that something like that could happen with an insurance company. We decided right then that this would be our next project.

"We made a sign that said we're going to raise fifteen thousand dollars. We organized the walkathon, and Megan Anderson's dad got us a car to raffle off. Pretty soon we said, 'Oh, we need to call People Helpers.' We got on the news, and before long the money started coming in. We probably passed fifteen thousand dollars in just a couple of hours.

"It was amazing, especially to be a ninth grader and see this stuff. Probably 80 to 90 percent of the class got involved in one way or another.

"I remember getting called out of class one time because the newspaper reporters were on the phone, wanting to talk to us. And I remember organizing and ordering the raffle tickets for the car. But I especially remember sitting with my friends in our living room helping to address the thank-you cards. We all got writer's cramp—there were probably five thousand cards. I remember saying, 'Print more cards. We're out.'

"It's emotional to go through that with your friends. To have your ten closest girlfriends in the room writing thank-yous for this sort of thing—you just bond. All of us are still best friends.

"It wasn't something that I chose to do. My heart said, 'This is what's right and this is what you're going to do.' God gives you these little walls in your life when you're a little kid. One little wall is making your bed by yourself. And then as you get older, the walls get big. But once they get knocked down, they become little walls. And next time you come against them it's so easy to go right over them. I think just realizing that you can knock down that wall opens up so many things. Now I find I can move through things so much easier. And I don't take no for an answer."

Chapter Twenty-seven

FINAL HURDLES

June 10, 12:30 P.M. I hold Michael as his eyelids begin to droop; the anesthesia is beginning to kick in. I think, "It's really going to happen!"

The perfect donor, Amy, is ready. The funds miraculously have become available. And now, Michael's surgery marks the third milestone in his treacherous road to recovery.

As Michael is wheeled in for surgery, Kristi and I sit in the hospital classroom where the nurse teaches us and other parents how to care for the Hickman catheter, otherwise known as "the line." It is the reason for Michael's surgery today.

We learn that one end of the long, narrow rubber tube will rest in the right atrium of Michael's heart. It travels up from the heart into the jugular vein, loops over the collarbone, submerges back under the skin another five inches, and exits with eighteen inches of tube protruding from his chest.

The line branches out into a Y; one end will be for intravenous feeding, the other for medications. For the next several months this lifeline will provide easy access for routine IVs, blood draws, and medications.

Besides the line, Michael is having tubes placed in his ears to eliminate his stubborn ear infections. In the meantime, Kristi and I are learning how to prevent any bacteria from infecting the entry site of the line. We must sterilize and cleanly dress it each day. We must secure it by wrapping it around his back and taping it down so he can't pull it out.

An hour later Michael comes out of surgery and into the recovery room, still asleep. Even with all he's been through, he seems so perfect. Now to have this long tube abnormally sticking out of our beautiful baby's chest in a way saddens and sickens us. But knowing what it eliminates makes it worth it. No more painful needle pokes into his fingers, arms, feet, legs, head, or anywhere else an untapped vein may be found! Fewer tears make it worth it.

Michael's neighbor in the cancer ward at Children's is a pretty, little, two-year-old girl, Jessica. She has a line, too, and a brain tumor.

Jan and Jerry, her parents, are about our age, with another child at home. Side by side in the hospital ward, we talk about our little ones and draw strength from an immediate bond.

We watch and learn as Jerry skillfully changes Jessica's Hickman dressing. Unknowingly they also challenge us. We must make a choice as parents: to focus on what we can do and pour ourselves into it, or focus on what we can't do and protectively shrink back into ourselves.

Courageous parents, Jan and Jerry pass the baton to us.

The Hickman line is just another hurdle in this long race. We learn we can only jump one at a time; we cannot worry about tomorrow.

From down the hall we hear the cries of a young mother.

She just got the tragic news. Their little boy is diagnosed with cancer. They too are forced to enter this race.

Tears and grief are the first painful steps in the healing process. Tears help to wash the wounded heart and prevent the infection of bitterness. The healing brought by time begins.

We pray for them—this child, these young parents. We think, "We know, we know. We're with you." We remember our first drive home from the hospital. Long months ago now, we arrived at the clinic and heard the hard facts from the doctor. We listened and asked questions, looking and acting as if we had it all together. Yet in the car, on the way home, we wept.

June 21. Father's Day. A marathon in Children's Hospital. Today is the nineteenth day in the last twenty-three that Michael has had to be hospitalized. Pneumonia is again the problem.

I sit alone with my son in his private room. Normally we would have switched today, but Kristi is sick at home with the flu. But this is where a daddy should be on Father's Day, under these circumstances. I'm exactly where I want to be—with a little one who needs me.

I wonder if God feels the same way on Father's Day. Does He want to be with His hurting child, with the ones who need Him most?

By God's strength, each moment is tolerable, each day another stride in an endurance race in which we must learn to pace ourselves. Childhood cancer is unquestionably a marathon.

Michael, despite it all, is so good, so happy, so content. All the nurses adore him. He is such a good patient, this beautiful little boy fighting to live.

The sad thing is that he doesn't know any different! To him, life means nothing but an unrelenting succession of fevers, pneumonia, labor-drawn breaths, chicken pox, ear infections, yeast infections, bruises, swollen liver and spleen, needles, IVs, transfusions, antibiotics, and sleepless nights. To him, life has always been a struggle.

And now, with para influenza virus attacking his lungs, the doctors debate: should they admit Michael directly to the Hutch or let him return home before the transplant? His ability to stay infection-free is questionable.

Our great, unspoken doubts tear at the deepest part of our souls. "Will we ever again tuck Michael into his own crib at night? Will we ever laugh at his funny faces at the dinner table again? Will we be a family together again?"

These accumulating hospital days weigh heavily upon Kristi. Not being able to nurse Michael anymore, not having him at home, and not having much control in her baby's life send pangs of discouragement deep in her mother-heart. Simple words, "Michael will be just fine," whispered by Brian Sternberg, a friend bound in a wheelchair for over thirty years, are a salve for her soul.

Wednesday, June 24. Two days without a fever! The doctors return with the verdict.

"We're going to let you take Michael home. The virus needs to run its course. He needs time to convalesce. Just be careful where you take him, and enjoy your baby for a few days."

"Thank You, Lord! Michael can come home! Thank You, God. He'll be home once more."

Getting him well is now the final obstacle in the race to the transplant.

An Interview With
Elisa Jaffe

Elisa was a reporter for KOMO *news in Seattle.*
She conducted an interview with the Leelands that prompted
an unprecedented response from the community.

"Everybody loved the story and said, 'We can't let go of this. This is a story we have to follow.' They wanted me to own it and to continue to watch Michael's progress. And, thank goodness, I can say 'progress' as opposed to 'deterioration.' At the time we didn't know which it was going to be.

"After the story aired, we got so many phone calls in the newsroom and so many letters that we realized we had opened a wound. We needed to give people the outlet they wanted—to see Michael all the time.

"By getting that story out there we saved a little boy's life. I went to a bank near Bothell where they took the donations, and I looked at check after check after check after letter after letter after card. I was sitting by the bank tellers and we were all crying. It was beautiful to see how many people were giving money they didn't even have. Later I went back to the Leelands' house and saw the whole family licking stamps— all the kids and their friends sitting around the table. Their tongues must have been tired!

"You expect that kind of reaction when there's a flood in the Midwest or a hurricane in Florida or you're raising food for the hungry and needy. You expect it when it's a huge thing that affects everybody. But you don't expect it when it's just one person's plight, when it's one family who has to raise that kind of money. That's what surprised me.

"Whenever you looked at Michael, it ripped your heart apart because you wanted to help this child and you couldn't imagine letting a little boy sit there and die because of bureaucracy.

"We just kept on looking at Michael's face; everybody was glued to the screen every time they saw his face. I think that's what kept us doing it. We felt for him. We felt for the whole family.

"This is one story that will always be with me, and I don't say that about a lot of stories. I've met many celebrities and politicians since then, but Michael had more impact on me than half the celebrities I've ever interviewed—which is interesting about a little boy who couldn't even talk."

Chapter Twenty-eight

A SMALL WINDOW
OF TIME

J une 25. We reconnect as a family and revel in the joy of being together. Savoring a little thing—time together—is like a gourmet meal. We take a family trip on the ferry-boat, play in the park, eat, laugh, shop. Our moments together, often taken for granted, are now made better intentionally.

And Michael is doing fantastic! When he's back home and doing well, it's so easy to believe, hope, pretend that everything is okay. "Maybe he doesn't really need the transplant. Maybe the doctors will find they made a mistake. Maybe God will heal Michael with a miracle."

We pray for a miracle.

June 30. Today marks Michael's first outpatient appointment at the Hutch, the Fred Hutchinson Cancer Research Center. High-risk patients come here from all over the world for expert care, yet the center is only thirty minutes from our home in Bothell. Divine intervention?

Michael goes in for blood tests and a physical. We get acquainted with Michael's new caregivers—different faces, new routines and quirks. Another adjustment. We miss the nurses and doctors at Children's Hospital, now like family.

The Hutch is both a research center and a place to care for very ill patients. We wonder about the research part; we definitely don't want our son to be a guinea pig for science.

Our initial trust is earned by the center's track record, but quickly we also sense the love coming from Michael's new nurses and doctors.

The cost of their caring is high. It is impossible not to get attached to the patients, all of whom share a need for the high-risk procedure. In order to endure, these caregivers must surely have learned to keep a looser grip on life and look at each day as a gift.

July 1. Michael needs his first transfusion of red blood cells. His counts have steadily been dropping, and his energy steadily decreases. The new blood cells take three hours to administer and give him a boost—as well as a fever.

Each day plods along during this week of appointments, more tests, long waits in between. We wonder, "When will the day come?" We feel we're stuck like an airplane in a holding pattern.

July 7. We are thankful that the last necessary tests are done today. They take an EKG of Michael's heart and one more bone marrow aspiration, a puncture to his pelvic bone. Another picture is taken to see if the enemy has gained ground—a recon report before the final battle plan is devised.

Again, we wait.

July 9. We are scheduled for a routine conference with the outpatient doctor to sign forms, get test results, and discuss Michael's treatment options. In preparation for this conference I arm myself with information. I intend to go to bat for Michael's best possible course of treatment. We definitely don't want the cure to be worse than the disease itself!

· So I study, research medical databases, and call a doctor at Berkeley who's an expert on Michael's rare condition. I search out the benefits and pitfalls of different regimens or protocols of treatment. What are the safest and most effective ways to eliminate the diseased cells?

What it takes, I find, is either intense chemotherapy or total body radiation—or sometimes, in the harder cases, both.

The tougher the regimen, the greater the disease-killing effect. Yet the tougher the regimen, the greater the risks of harmful side effects.

We learn that the least amount of chemo, by itself, will render our boy sterile and possibly stunt his growth. We fear the potential damage that radiation can do to other vital organs, especially in our developing baby. We're driven to learn the long-term impact of these life-saving decisions... and to consider the grief of him losing the ability to have his own children. With our thoughts racing into tomorrow, our hearts can only rest in hope beyond it.

July 9, 11:20 A.M. Kristi and I have been waiting for fifteen minutes for the doctor. Suddenly she enters the small meeting room, quickly greets us, then point-blank unloads her arsenal. She has the results of the bone marrow test taken two days ago.

"Michael's marrow is packed with blasts [bad cells]," she states objectively. "He is now in transition to acute leukemia."

Our hearts sink with her words. She is very forthright and recommends the most intense regimen for Michael.

"Our plan," she continues, "is to give him six days of high-dose chemotherapy and then six days of total body radiation."

Kristi and I sit in silence, still trying to absorb the first blows.

A twelve-day course of chemo and radiation. What will that do to Michael? Will the cure be worse than the disease? Can we really trust this doctor?

"Are you sure about this?" we ask. "What about the side effects?" I cannot help but think, *Please don't make our baby an experiment!* "If Michael were your son," I ask, "would you do the same thing?"

"Michael's number one risk," she replies, now with a tone of compassion, "is to have this disease come back. That is his greatest risk, not the damage to his body." She pauses, then adds, "By the way, can you have him back here by one o'clock? We want Michael admitted today."

"Today!"

"Yes. I'm also recommending he be placed in LAF."

We've heard and read about these sterile isolation rooms. Since Michael had a related, perfectly matched donor, we thought he wouldn't need it.

"Because of Michael's high risk, I think this would be best for him. We'll show you a videotape on it in a few minutes."

"Whatever you think," we answer softly. By now we have run out of ammo. We weren't expecting this today.

We rush home to get Michael and hurriedly pack. When we get to the house a half hour later, we take time to pray together as a family. We cuddle and let the kids say goodbye to baby brother.

It's the hardest goodbye ever.

We are no longer able to put off the thought, *Will Michael ever come home again?* How easy it would be not to go back today, to keep our Michael home with us, to pretend everything is okay.

Should we really put him through this? Our baby! How can we?

"It's after one o'clock. We have to get going," I hear myself saying.

We leave the kids, wiping away tears. We force ourselves to remember that we do this to help Michael get better. Yet we know he must first get much worse.

An Interview With
Mike and Karen Rohrbach
Mike and Karen are close friends of Jeff and Kristi.

"The Leelands' oldest child and our oldest child are five weeks apart. The next oldest in our families are four months apart. The next two are nine days apart, and the last two are two months apart," says Karen. "So every time we would call them up and say, 'Guess what? We're pregnant,' they'd say, 'Well, guess what? We are, too!' "

"We've been close friends for a long time, but when we found out such bad news, our feeling was helplessness," says Mike, one of Jeff's former teammates at the University of Washington. "What can you do? In a sense, I didn't know what to do as a friend. We could pray; we could encourage. But there was this fear. When we thought of our own children—especially with our kids being so close in age to theirs—we were thankful we weren't going through it personally. And yet we felt so connected because of our friendship and the special times we've had over the years. We really didn't know what to do. Then we thought of Evon.

"Evon is a college student and friend of both families."

"It was interesting how it all turned out," Karen says. "Mike and I had been discussing the fact that Jeff and Kristi would have to spend a lot of time at the hospital all summer. What were they going to do with their kids? It was a terrible burden to put on his parents, and to cart them from one place to another every day would be hard on the kids. So I said, 'It's too bad we couldn't find somebody who could stay at their house.' After we went to bed one night, I woke up suddenly at two o'clock, and it just hit me: Evon! We knew her, they knew her. It worked out for Evon to move in with us so that she could take care of the Leeland kids for the summer while they were at the hospital a lot. It was neat."

"It was neat," Mike agrees, then adds, "but we didn't do anything heroic."

Chapter Twenty-nine

SAYING GOODBYE

A television crew waits for us at the main entrance of Swedish Hospital as we arrive with Michael. The Fred Hutchinson Cancer Research Center is across the street and leases out the two top floors of this hospital—10 and 11 Southwest—as bone marrow transplant units. With the camera in our faces, we carry Michael to the hallways of 10 Southwest, the pediatric transplant floor.

The news team is given permission to be there by Susan, the Hutch media coordinator. She will be our buffer between reporters and cameras in the days and weeks ahead.

But today is a celebration. It is a come-from-behind win for Michael, an incredible team effort, a community's victory. Many people have a vested interest in this story; they own a piece of Michael's life. All of them increase our joy and share our pain.

We walk off the elevator and are met by Phuong, the admitting nurse. Then we are taken on a tour. First stop, room 1015. Like a penthouse suite, Michael's tenth floor room faces west on Capitol Hill, offering a panoramic view of the beautiful, downtown Seattle skyline set against the deep blue of Puget Sound. Like any hospital room, this one is quite functional and sanitary, with nothing posh about the clinical decor.

Continuing the tour of the floor, we find it a virtual mini-hospital, with its own kitchen, pharmacy, supply rooms, nurses' stations, conference rooms, and offices. Next we see the family lounge, featuring a kitchen, sofas, TV, and a play area for siblings. Designed as a place of respite and fellowship for burden bearers, it is also a place for weary friends and relatives.

The other two hallways border the patient rooms and merge with three intensive care units—places we hope never to see—and a waiting room in the corner between.

The waiting room. Our final stop for a meeting with staff members, attending doctor, social worker, and nurses before Michael is admitted. The conference is a description of life on 10 Southwest.

We are told what we can expect in the weeks to follow, informed of available resources, and advised of decisions we must make about optional experimental studies and treatments. Finally we are briefed on the major risks Michael will face and his prognosis.

The bottom line.

"Jeff and Kristi," explains Dr. Smith, "based on Michael's condition, he has a 45 percent chance of survival."

Essentially, if our hopes rest entirely in this treatment, it's a coin toss between life and death.

"But if successful," he adds, "it's likely to mean a lifetime cure."

Without it, incurable leukemia and death. With it…life?

The enormity of it all—the severity and length of the

process, the finality and weight of the outcome—is over-whelming.

"Michael's room is now being prepared," the doctor says. "Why don't you take a walk with your boy and come back in half an hour?"

In thirty minutes Michael will be placed in sterile isola-tion. A plastic barrier from infection will soon separate us. Called a "LAF" room, short for "laminar air flow" room, it is designed for higher risk patients undergoing a bone marrow transplant.

A final half-hour with our son. A few last moments together for mother, father, and child. A few moments to touch him, moments to carry us through the many anxious weeks to come. Weeks will pass before we can hope to kiss and hold him again…if ever again.

It is a cherished time, an agonizing time.

It is a time to say goodbye.

An Interview With
Susan Edmonds

*Susan works as the media relations manager
at the Fred Hutchinson Cancer Research Center in Seattle.
She gave medical updates on Michael and arranged
for TV crews to witness the transplant.*

"The very first contact I had with the family was when I heard about the fund-raising. When I saw the picture of Michael that QFC, the grocery store chain, put in the paper, I actually cut it out and put it on my wall. I knew then that they would do well.

"Every family's a little different in how they deal with the media. There were a lot of demands, of course, to see Michael and the family. We tried to spread it out so it wasn't overwhelming and so it wouldn't interfere with the process. In order for any crew to go on the floor, we have to go through the normal checks system and make sure the doctors are comfortable with it.

"It was really interesting with Michael. Regardless of what day of the transplant process it was, when we would go up on the floor, he was always smiling, always photogenic. He's just a cute kid. I can't imagine him being cranky because I've never seen him cranky.

"What was different about Michael is who he was while he was going through the transplant. He was so personable that people just naturally migrated to him."

Chapter Thirty

LETTING GO

The warm July sun sends gentle breezes playing through Michael's downy soft hair. Kristi and I kiss his face over and over again as we sit in the park in front of the Research Center.

These are cherished moments on the edge of uncertainty with our ten-month-old boy.

In the next twelve days, Michael's existing marrow will be destroyed, the good cells along with the bad. And within the pelvic bones of his seven-year-old sister, Amy, precious, perfectly matched "stem cells" await transplant. Amy will soon be the brave, loving donor of her own bone marrow, possibly saving her brother's life.

Tomorrow Michael will begin his journey. Six days of high-dose chemotherapy and six more days of intense, total body radiation await him, a pre-transplant regimen to purge his small body of diseased cells. A regimen which will also lead him down a path into extreme vulnerability.

Michael will soon face the high risks of life-threatening complications, running the gamut from common infection and toxic damage to his organs, to "graft-versus-host disease" (GVHD), in which Amy's transplanted white cells would reject and attack Michael's organs.

The doctor only minutes ago made sure that we carried no false hopes into this high-tech, low-touch procedure which gives our boy only a 45 percent "chance" of survival.

Foreseeing our baby's time of tremendous suffering is a burden now too heavy to bear. What can we say or do to convey our love to Michael as these last moments together quickly pass?

We kiss and nuzzle him, wondering if he remembers the pain of his other hospital stays. Will he be afraid behind the LAF barrier? What if he cries out for his mother's warm touch? How will we comfort him? How will we communicate our love?

The answer to these questions, we are convinced, must rest in the hands of the same loving God who already has shown His ability to turn tragedy into triumph. Once again we must simply trust Him and let go.

By four o'clock we are wiping the tears from our eyes. Weak-kneed, we return to the room with Michael. These are not butterflies in my stomach—they feel more like a swarm of locusts eating away my strength. I struggle for the intestinal fortitude even to ride the elevator back upstairs.

I whisper a prayer with each step. For the moment I am given strength, just enough to put one foot in front of the other.

We have discovered along our hard journey two kinds of hope. One looks forward to the final destination, the other looks for the strength and wisdom to move toward it. Both rest in God's faithful provision.

We have also encountered two types of discouragement. One mistakes an obstacle in the path for the final destination; the other mistakes our own weakness for a reason to give up. Both rest in our faithlessness.

Room 1015, just another step in our journey. Here we find a nurse preparing sterile bathwater in a small plastic tub.

"Hi, I'm Jenny!"

"Hi," Kristi responds, "we're Jeff and Kristi."

"It's so nice to meet you! And, Michael—what a sweetheart you are!"

Our tension melts in the warmth of her caring spirit.

I enter the room and scan the transparent wall which will separate us from our child. The front half of the LAF room will be for us, the back for Michael. We will be isolated from our son by a barrier made of glass and a clear, plastic curtain. The only entrance is an opening with pure, filtered air blowing out of it. Like a shield for handling nuclear waste, two plastic arm sleeves with rubber gloves penetrate the curtain and reach into Michael's crib on the other side.

This is LAF, a sterile refuge from the outside world, a technological substitute for the human immune system.

This separation, so necessary for Michael's protection, nevertheless presents an emotional paradox for his parents. It prevents the touch of death by isolating our baby from opportunistic microorganisms, yet it denies the touch of life. The price of rubber gloves and a sterile mask is the loss of a warm caress, a gentle kiss.

"If you want to give Michael his bath before he goes into LAF," Jenny says, "I'll gown up and go in. Then you can hand him across to me."

Only an arm's length away. It tears our hearts in two.

We bathe our son. We slowly run our fingers through

his fine hair, knowing it will soon be gone. A squiggle. A giggle. We make a memory.

We wash his weak little body with special soap, cleansing him to enter his sterile sanctuary. It is a baptism in warm, pure water.

We dry him, cuddle him, then wrap him in a warm, sterile blanket.

At five o'clock on July 9 we release our baby across the invisible boundary into the hands of Jenny. We commit our baby Michael into the hands of God. With no strings attached.

An Interview With
Nurse Candy

*Nurse Candy has spent many years on the pediatric transplant
floor of the Fred Hutchinson Cancer Research Center.
She developed a special bond with Michael's family
during his ordeal.*

"What we do at the beginning is introduce the family to their
child's environment, how you get food made in the kitchen,
the family room, where to get a cot—just how they live here.
Then we start introducing people. They come in, one after
another, from different departments. The nutritionist sees
them, we see them, the doctors see them. It's back-to-back
introductions the first day.

"From there, usually on the same day, we put them into
the LAF room, the sterile room. Before a patient goes in, we
have to do a decontamination bath. The family is usually
involved in helping with that elaborate process. The parents
have to understand how to get the child prepared and
cleaned, how to live in a sterile environment, what you can
and can't touch.

"I knew the story of the Leelands' fund-raising from
watching Michael's parents on TV. Just from watching them,
I had the feeling they were really a happy group. They had
taken what was going on with the insurance, but they
weren't fighting it; they just went from there. And knowing
that, you wanted to have contact with them. We all wanted
to, even before we saw Michael's picture. When we finally
saw him, we all went, 'Now we really want to!'

"Michael was adorable every minute. He would stand up

by the edge of the crib and look out through the plastic wall when you'd walk in the room to take care of him. If you had put black, round glasses on him, he would have looked exactly like Mr. Magoo. Remember Mr. Magoo? The little cartoon character who was always walking around with his bald head, looking at everything? Michael looked just like him, so I called him Mr. Magoo. And it stuck."

Chapter Thirty-one

DEEPER FAITH

Tonight it is my turn to stay at Michael's side, the first of many alternating twenty-four-hour shifts for Kristi and me.

Reaching through the curtain, Kristi hugs her baby in arms of clear plastic. Rubber-covered hands blow him a kiss goodbye. She hugs me; we pray together, then kiss good-bye.

Kristi—a quietly courageous, tenderhearted, dedicated mother with the love of Jesus in her heart. She grieves inwardly, rarely expressing it except upon my shoulder—quietly, together, alone. A father and mother intimately connected by an incredible heartache. She goes home to relieve Evon, a college student and friend of the family, who will be a nanny for Jaclyn, Amy, and Kevin this summer, thanks to our friends the Rohrbachs and their church, Antioch Alliance.

The children miss Michael—and Kristi and me. They experience pangs of separation no less real, no less intense, but often less communicated and less understood than our own. We pray that Evon's familiar face will somehow be a comforting presence in our absence.

Michael and I are now alone at the very precipice of this deep, dark canyon. It is far steeper and more treacherous than anything we've ever faced. Father and child, we are separated by the wall between us.

A deep longing for intimacy creates a void within me. Only through the healing lifeblood of a sibling may this chasm now be bridged. Restoring this little one back to wholeness, back into face-to-face relationship, is the great passion of my heart.

Michael is fed and falls asleep by eight o'clock. Everything so far goes smoothly. Strangely, I sense he is not alone. I watch through the plastic curtain as he rests, comfortably and content. And I sense something else—that he senses he is not alone. The thought comforts me enough to leave him for a little while to get some dinner myself.

I know the emptiness inside me will not be satisfied with food, so eating tonight is an exercise of discipline, not pleasure. I return to the room a little while later, to lay out the reclining chair, then my sleeping bag, and last my body. I am exhausted and must get some rest.

Yet it will not be easy. Emotions continue to billow like agitated waves that need time to settle down after the day's storm has passed. Into my Father's lap I climb, a place of solitude and security.

"Dear God, hold me in Your arms. Quiet the troubled waters of my soul."

Be still, and know that I am God.

I find safe harbor for the night, a deeper calmness for my soul. These still waters give the best reflections.

In these reflections I'm shown brief glimpses of the front side, the eternal side, of this tapestry called life. The Master

Weaver in wisdom and skill blends each thread into perfect place, using even the dark threads of suffering and pain to create an awesomely beautiful tapestry. Yet this picture is hard to appreciate from our temporal point of view.

In reflection, however, I see grace. Grace dispensed on a moment-by-moment basis, at exactly the point of true need. Such grace is manifested in many overlooked ways: the visit of a friend, a dinner left at our doorstep, the warmth of a nurse, a word of encouragement. Sadly, it is grace we often miss when our heart demands things which are not needed, things not for the best.

Reflections eventually turn into projections. I find myself asking, *Can I face tomorrow with confidence in the face of bad news today?*

The conferences, reports of Michael's rapidly advancing leukemia, a poor prognosis, requirements of intense chemo and radiation, rushing him in with so little warning, releasing him from our arms to the isolation of LAF—how can I sleep peacefully tonight, knowing the things that really matter in life are the things I control the least? How can I rest with the future of my baby boy hanging in the balance, out of my hands?

A simple answer keeps ringing in my mind: *only in child-like faith.*

Such a faith approaches God as a loving Father, not as some kind of prayer-operated vending machine. This is a faith that finds more pleasure in the grasp of His hand than in some handout. It is a faith that seeks first a relationship with Him before the results I desperately desire.

I cannot control the future. I do not know all that the future holds. But, yes, I can confidently face tomorrow. I can go to sleep tonight because I do know who holds the future in His hands. I know He is the One who will withhold something good only in order to give His child what is best. I know He is the One with limitless power, with infinite goodness, who will do abundantly more than I can ever ask or imagine.

10:30 P.M. I curl up in my sleeping bag. Michael is snug in his crib. We both are resting in the arms of God, our Father.

> *I will lie down and sleep in peace,*
> *for you alone, O LORD,*
> *make me dwell in safety.*

PSALM 4:8

An Interview With
Mike and Mary Baldassin
Mike and Mary are close friends of Jeff and Kristi.

"From the beginning, we thought, 'This is a mountain. It's an uphill climb, and it's going to be a slow process.' Yet it was amazing how funds came in so quickly and how the kids at Kamiakin got into it. People rallied. It's as if they came out of the woodwork.

"We knew God was in control and that He could use us and others to help Michael," Mike says. "Still, it surprised me that funds came in so quickly and in such large amounts. From a natural standpoint, you'd say this was a fluke, a one-time thing. But as Christians we looked at it and said, 'No, this is God's will; this is how He's going to pull it off.' It was an affirmation that God really is in control, that He was somehow going to work this out through others.

"It was difficult to walk down the floor at the Hutch and see others in a similar situation to Michael's and know that as soon as we left the doors of that building, everything was safe outside in our own home, yet just yards behind us there was grief and suffering. Sometimes we felt it wasn't fair that Jeff and Kristi should have to go through this—or anyone else for that matter. Why are they having to go through this and not us or someone else?

"We needed to help. People are vulnerable in that setting. They need a hand; they need love and reassurance."

Chapter Thirty-two

THE DOWNHILL PATH

A wakened at half past four in the morning by the rustling of the plastic curtain, I reorient myself to the hospital room. Through the dim light I see a nurse changing Michael's diaper and drawing blood samples from his Hickman line.

She works through the curtain, caring for our baby through the transparent wall of a sterile barrier. The reality of this image shakes me awake *to* a nightmare, rather than *from* one.

Michael's countdown really begins today, Friday, July 10. "Day minus 12" on the clinical calendar, a day of hope, a day of dread. His journey begins down a most treacherous path—the descent to a zero immune system.

Chemo and radiation will be his deadly escorts to July 21, "Day 0." That day Amy's marrow will be given him, a lifeline to carry him back up the other side. We hope.

How long will he be here? This is definitely no quick fix. The grueling descent and treacherous climb back up will take two months in the hospital, a year in recovery. The only other option to this painful pathway? A free fall into leukemia. A dead end.

Even though Michael walks through this valley of the shadow of death, we know our little lamb has a Good Shepherd, One who will lead and comfort him, One who will never leave or forsake him. The Lord is with him. And yet....

Every item Michael needs for his journey—food, diapers, pajamas, blankets, medical supplies, toys—must be sterilized. Everything he will touch will have to be carefully relayed to him: specially sterilized, wrapped, and transferred with tongs through the air barrier doorway, this cumbersome curtain which will shield him from our affection as well.

One at a time we, too, may enter Michael's sterile haven for short periods by adapting ourselves to his environment. Jenny demonstrates the ritual we must learn if we want to approach Michael, just as the doctors and nurses do.

We watch as she systematically dons the decontaminated attire. Shoes off, hands washed, face masked, head covered. She carries a package to the narrow LAF entryway. Wrapped inside are clothlike paper garments: knee-high boots and a full-length gown.

She flips the switch on the wall marked "Blower," and instantly a stiff breeze of purified air pushes through the entryway. The built-in, wall-sized air filtration system gives merit to the name, "laminar air flow" room.

We watch as Jenny slowly unwraps the first layer of paper. Like an onion peel, another layer beneath it contains a gown and boots. She slides the bundle up to the red line on the floor and slowly unfolds it. With wind in her face, Jenny uses a pair of tongs from a stainless steel container of alcohol to pick up the boots. As she shakes them, they unfold. Each foot must be independently placed down on the white paper after the boot is slipped on. A balancing act in dressing!

"You have to be careful," she warns. "If the garments touch anything, throw them away and start over."

What an ordeal! we think.

Next, the inside-out gown is picked up and shaken open. Jenny's arms slip into the sleeves. Meticulously, she tucks her fingers into the surgical gloves, using one to carefully pull on the other and stretching them over her cuffs. Finally, she reaches around her back to tie the gown. Now completely covered—mummified except for a narrow patch of skin around her eyes—Jenny steps from the paper, across the red line, and into the LAF.

An Interview With
Kristi Leeland
Kristi is Michael's mom.

"The most difficult time for me in the whole ordeal was handing our baby over, having to release him into the care and trust of others behind that screen. That was the hardest—not being able to touch him. I'm a snuggler, I like to cuddle, and Michael was used to that. He was used to a lot of contact. And suddenly I couldn't touch him. We had to be very careful about bringing in germs. Maybe we had a cold coming on and didn't know it. That was scary—probably the scariest part. Not knowing.

"What helped me the most during that whole period was spending time in prayer and spending time in the Word. A sense of peace just came upon me. Jeff's attitude during the whole thing was also calming. When parents go through something like this, it can either tear them apart or draw them closer together. We drew a lot closer. I think our whole family did, even the kids. God really is faithful."

Chapter Thirty-three

PAINFUL CONNECTIONS

Our baby's natural life-support system gradually erodes. His only umbilical cord to the outside world now is the Hickman line implanted in his heart, extending from his chest, and penetrating through the protective walls of his new sterilized womb: LAF. He is totally dependent upon the blood supplied by outside donors and the perfectly balanced, intravenous diet to survive.

Tubes, chemotherapy treatments, radiation bouts. The "nasal-gastric feeding tube" becomes the newest connection. As the name implies, the tube bypasses the mouth. Our baby gags, fights, and cries as the "NG" tube is run up his nose, down his throat, and into his stomach. Not a pleasant way to ingest something, yet it spares him the nauseating taste of oral chemotherapy.

Michael shows his style as a fighter, launching sneak attacks on the tube. He pulls out four, and four are replaced. He wins a few battles, but loses the tube war.

His now highly toxic urine can damage his bladder and kidneys. So after four days the "NG" permanently comes out, and another tube is pushed up into him to drain the contaminated, chemotherapy runoff.

July 16. The downhill path continues with a new escort. Baby Michael is wrapped, masked, and transported in a wagon to a lead-lined room. The first day of total body radiation has come.

The first bout lasts a half-hour. It is repeated six more days, and each day Michael takes another step closer to the transplant, yet another step downhill.

A step forward, a step backward. Each dose a blessing and a curse. Radiation and chemo do their work with the effectiveness and precision of a napalm bomb.

With anticipation we watch the figures each day as Michael's blood counts drop steadily lower and lower. Like battlefield body counts, they show the enemy leukemic cells being destroyed.

We also watch as he suffers the inevitable side effects of good cells destroyed by "friendly fire." Michael's beautiful blond, baby hair is the first to go; we must shave it off. His appetite is next. He stops eating and drinking entirely. The tender membranes of his digestive tract, from his mouth all the way to his bottom, are blasted, burned, and blistered along with all the other fast-dividing cells. The bombardment leaves a swollen mouth on one end and the most incredible diaper rash on the other, with no white cells to bring healing.

This is so difficult! And at the same time humbling and inspiring. A little one so tender, so helpless—one moment nauseated to the point of internal bleeding, the next feebly pulling himself up by the side rail of the crib and smiling at us through the plastic curtain.

What might he be thinking?

We continue to build friendships on 10 Southwest. We touch wounded souls, other parents carrying other tremendous burdens. We build bridges with fellow travelers who are walking in shoes even heavier than our own.

One couple carries the weight of their precious little one on their heart as he clings to life in intensive care. Together we lean on God. Together we pray—and cry.

Medical technology opens a Pandora's box, bringing great possibilities but ever tougher decisions. Artificial connections to life abound: respirators, heart machines, tubes.

One set of parents painfully senses the inevitable...and disconnects the chain that was once a lifeline.

An Interview With
Jaclyn Leeland
Jaclyn is Michael's eldest sister.

"I remember the day we found out. We were in the living room, and all of a sudden Mom started crying. She came in, and we said, 'What's wrong?' Every time Michael got a fever over a hundred, he'd have to go to the hospital. That day he had a fever. So Mom had to call a pediatrician.

"In some ways it was kind of fun at first when Michael was in the hospital because we didn't have to do school. But it wasn't fun having Mom and Dad gone and Michael sick all the time.

"I cried the night Michael went into the hospital for his transplant, the day before he started chemo. I was thinking, 'What if Michael dies?' I didn't think he would, but it could happen; it could really happen.

"Later, I'd go in to see Michael with Dad or Mom once or twice a week. One time I got dressed up in the sterile gown, and I went in and got to hold him and give him his bottle and everything. That was fun.

"But it was not fun being on TV. I didn't like being on TV. I thought I looked weird, or didn't do anything right. I tried to stay off it as much as I could."

Chapter Thirty-four

GOOD DAYS

E ven on the pediatric transplant floor there are good days, blessed days that no parent here can ever take for granted.

It's a good day when you wake up in a reclining chair, feeling strangely refreshed, realizing your child slept peacefully through the night as well. It's a good day when there are no chemotherapy or radiation treatments for your baby to undergo, when a blood transfusion has not brought on fever or chills, when the nauseating but necessary oral antibiotics stay down. No surprises, no fevers, no signs of infection, no congested lungs, no painful tears—these are the ingredients of truly good days.

Having the kids up to see their little brother on Sunday after church makes a good day. When he stands up to the rail of his crib and smiles as each takes a turn reaching through the curtain, stroking him with rubber gloves. Yes, this has become a good day.

Good news on the floor helps make it a good day. Another boy's new marrow engrafts! A little one has made it out of intensive care! The baby girl next door will soon be discharged to go home! Hope makes for a good day.

Dinner out with your wife, alone—this makes it a very good day.

A friend calls you on the phone. Someone cares enough to stop by and visit. With an arm around your shoulder someone offers a prayer, even though words are hard to come by.

Yes, even here, good days can be found.

An Interview With
Kevin Leeland

*Kevin is Michael's older brother. He was almost four
years old when Michael had the transplant.*

"Michael got sick and then he got a bone marrow transplant. And when I went to the hospital, the clown was there. He had a brown jacket and patches on. He gave me stickers and stuff. I played with the tricycles in the hallway, and we played in the wheelchairs. And I played in the playroom with books and toys and trucks.

"Michael's room was like putting gloves through the window. Dad dressed up into a hospital-man. Then he held Michael.

"Amy was his donor. She saved Michael's life by getting her blood into Michael's blood so he wouldn't die.

"I think Amy was special."

Chapter Thirty-five

DAY ZERO

July 21, 6 A.M. We have reached the crux of this journey toward healing.

On the way to the hospital a young girl finally opens up. "Mommy…" Amy says, "do I have to do this? Is there anybody else that can?"

"Amy, this is something only you can choose to do. Only you can help save Michael's life today."

With a tear still in her eye at the prospect of pain, the extraordinary warmth of Amy's heart triumphs over her cold feet. "Okay."

Love overcomes fear.

With Michael's marrow now destroyed, seven-year-old Amy carries life for two in her bones—a big reason for us to have been a bit overprotective the past few weeks. This was the reason she was left behind when Jaclyn and Kevin got to cross the state to their Uncle Greg and Aunt Wendy's lake place—another sacrifice she admirably accepted with a hint of disappointment but no complaints.

Amy's surgery will occur at eight o' clock. She will be put under and be fully asleep by the time her lower back is punctured numerous times with a long, thick needle that will draw out rich, bloodlike marrow from her pelvic bones to be stored in a sterile IV bag. She will need only a few days in the hospital to recuperate from surgery, but it will take a few weeks to rebuild her strength from lost marrow.

7:30 A.M. Michael slept well last night, even though the radiation has compounded the effects of chemo, making him more tired and nauseated than ever before. Thank goodness his last treatment is this morning.

The nurse, like a little girl with her doll, gives Michael a final wagon ride to the lead-lined room. His eyes peep from between the oversized cap and face mask he must wear as he is wheeled into the elevator, totally wrapped up in a sterile, protective cocoon.

The radiation room is painted orange and furnished, almost humorously, to look like a living room—stereo, TV, paintings, lamps. And two monster-sized, cobalt, X-ray machines standing at both ends of the room. In the middle, the small, wooden crib lined with Plexiglas will contain our little boy for a last 31.8 minute push down into the valley.

The heavy doors close behind us as we watch Michael by means of a video camera in the technician's room. The invisible rays silently bombard his tiny body one last time. He slowly dozes off in little-boy slumber.

8:30 A.M. Michael returns to the LAF room, still sleeping. We receive word that Amy's marrow is out. The surgery went well. She is doing fine, still unconscious in the recovery room.

"Thank You, God."

A phone call comes from Susan, the media coordinator. Television cameras are coming up to record the start of the transplant for the evening news. We attempt to stay out of the way as the pace in the room steps up a notch.

Time is not wasted with these precious, new marrow cells. The transplant will begin soon and will take seven hours to complete.

Today's amazing procedure is as incredibly simple as it is simply miraculous. There is no intricate or lengthy surgery for Michael as I first envisioned. These microscopic "blood factories" will travel from the IV bag into the line in Michael's heart. If the transplant is successful, within three weeks Amy's cells will have found their own way "home" into Michael's bones. They will "engraft" and begin regenerating. Then, we hope, they will begin producing a new breed of compatible lifeblood, a new immune system, and a new disease-free, baby boy.

The greatest difficulties hide in the long, "pre" and "post" stage processes of the bone marrow transplant. Michael's body is being subjected to the effects of destroying the old cells and to two months of virtually no blood production, no immune system, and no oral intake of food. Now, finally, he must withstand the introduction of aggressive, new immune cells which, no matter how compatible, are still likely to attack.

Kristi and I watch Michael's primary nurse, Sandy, skill-fully work with the large rubber gloves through the curtain, connecting another transparent tube to Michael, threading it through the small port in the plastic wall and back to the tall tower of eight IV pumps. From one of them hangs Amy's bone marrow.

The television crew arrives just as Sandy is hooking up the bag of Amy's marrow to Michael's IV. We're interviewed from this vantage point, realizing in this moment our little boy has reached the crucial point of his journey.

It is a moment more properly reserved for unspeakable reverence than for manufactured TV exuberance, but the latter must be permitted. It's hard to know what to say.

At long last, it's happening! Seeing the bright crimson fluid slowly wind its way through the seven-foot-long IV tubing, then penetrate the plastic curtain and go into Michael's Hickman line, and finally enter his heart, we are overwhelmed. Words do not come easily, and they are unnecessary.

After months of hardship and grace, pain and joy, fear and hope, we feel an overpowering, consuming love for our children. We have at last stepped out of this valley and onto the road toward healing. The precious blood of a sibling has provided our son's only lifeline back.

Now we wait, longing for his return.

An Interview With
Amy Leeland
Amy is Michael's older sister.
She became his "perfect" bone marrow match.

"I was sad when I found out Michael was sick. I remember we had to stay all day at the hospital. We waited and waited until Mom came out.

"The day I found out I had something that would help Michael we were all playing outside, and Mom called us from the hospital. Grandma was there, and she gave me the phone, and Mom told me. Then Grandma called everybody else in. She said, 'I know who's the donor,' and everybody guessed. Jaclyn goes, 'Kevin?' and I go, 'No.' And she says, 'Me?' and I go, 'No.' And she goes, 'You?' and I said 'Yes.' It made me feel good.

"That was a really fun time because Jaclyn and Kevin went for a week to Wapato Point. It was just me at home, and I got paid a lot of attention. I had to stay home because I was the donor. I got to do lots of things—I got to do whatever I wanted because there was nobody else who wanted to do anything else.

"I was scared the morning of the transplant. I told Mama I wanted her to stay by me the whole time. Then I woke up and I was really tired. I tried to sit up, but they didn't want me to because of my back. I had to have lots of fruit. It was fun being in the hospital because I got my own phone and my own TV. And it was special for Michael. When he gets a little older, I'll tell him that I saved his life."

Chapter Thirty-six

EMOTIONAL
ROLLER COASTER

J uly 31. The late afternoon sun beams through the large
picture window, causing me to sweat under the sterile layers of clothing demanded in the LAF. This scene has
become a daily ritual.

"Would you like to try to give something to Michael to
eat?" Dean, the cook, raises his voice enough for me to hear
through the plastic curtain and over the gentle hum of the
air filtration system. Even the food going into the LAF must
be specially prepared and packaged.

"How about some applesauce?" I ask. My voice, muffled
by the face mask, carries a tone of optimism, although
Michael hasn't swallowed food in many days. This time is no
different.

It's Day plus 10—ten days since the transplant. We wait,
doing everything possible in the meantime to nurse Michael
back to health, yet knowing he must pass three mileposts
before he'll ever reach home again. The "Big Three":

- being without infection or fever;
- eating well;
- having neutrophil (white cell) counts over 500.

Baby steps for most children. Giant leaps for Michael.

Inasmuch as the sterile environment has helped keep Michael infection-free, it has been worth the price of separation and extra work. Kristi and I have become quite proficient at gowning up, going in, and doing as many nursing tasks as possible. Any task that draws us near to our son, even temporarily, is a labor of love.

Four times a day we sterilize him, inside and out, with medications. Because he has trouble swallowing, we trick Michael by slipping the plastic, medicating syringe in with his pacifier to get the antibiotics down. Powders and creams are applied to all his little bodily cracks and orifices to kill off bacteria and fungus. Finally, we sterilely bathe and change Michael's Hickman dressing once a day.

Having spent nearly a month in this room, we can now sleep through Michael's blood draws at 4:30 A.M., oblivious to the rustling curtain only a few feet away. Since Day minus 12, Michael's first day in the hospital, the results of the blood draw have provided the numerical map which charts Michael's transplant trek. First it marked the downhill path, showing his white cells falling to zero. Since Day 0 we've begun to look for signs of the upward trail. We long for any indication of white counts: the first signs of engraftment, the production of new cells.

A simple chart on the wall records Michael's progress (or lack of it). These numbers now reveal his ever increasing need for donated platelets and red blood cells—care packages given for his survival while he struggles through hostile territory.

As each morning passes, we find ourselves more anxiously awaiting the 10:30 A.M. results of this one simple test.

We pray against the dark forces of infirmity which might attack him at any moment in this vulnerable state. And we wait.

Saturday, August 1, Day +11. Today the sign appears, 11 days post-transplant. Michael has counts...110! "Thank You, God!"

But disappointment follows.

Sunday, Day +12...40.
Monday, Day +13...80.
Tuesday, Day +14...100.
Wednesday, Day +15...130.
Thursday, Day +16...160. He's climbing!
Friday, Day +17...150. One step back.
Saturday, Day +18...150.
Sunday, Day +19...230. A big jump!
Only to fall again. Monday, Day +20...130.
Tuesday, August 11, Day +21, dropping to...0.

What's happening? Is the transplant not working? Could the new marrow be failing?

The doctors and nurses cautiously reassure us that progress can be slow, sometimes up and down. Yet we sense their quiet concern as well.

Within the next week, Michael's counts peak and valley two more times, reaching once above 450, then twice again below 150. Our hearts are lifted up and then come crashing down on a roller coaster of hope and disappointment, following the jagged line of the chart. The higher our hopes, the harder we fall. We long for that elusive count of 500. Oh, how we long to hold our baby again!

The platelet transfusions from the blood bank become
less and less effective, more and more frequent. Kristi and I
are called on to give our platelets because the boost from a
related donor is usually better. Each day that Michael goes
without white cells increases the opportunity the enemy has
to mount a life-threatening attack.

We grow weary in waiting, knowing our little boy lives
on borrowed time. Time now apart from us.

Nonetheless, this situation forces us to refocus our eyes
on simple truths:

taking one day at a time;

handing to God what we cannot control;

pouring our hearts into what we can;

thanking Him for the results.

An Interview With
Dixie Rasmussen
Dixie is Kristi's mother.

"The first thing I was really concerned about was: Where would they find a match? And I was concerned about the transplant; you hear all these stories about chemo and radiation.

"The first time I went up to the hospital was scary. But Michael was really good. The only time he put up a fuss was when he went to have radiation by himself and no one could go into the room with him. Thirty minutes of total body radiation was a lot! His little bottom was just blistered, and he didn't want to have his diaper changed because it hurt.

"I was also concerned about the other kids. I don't think they really understood why their mother and father had to pay so much attention to Michael or why they had to have a baby-sitter. I think Kevin in particular didn't understand why his mother wasn't there.

"I was concerned for Kristi too. She was absolutely worn out. She spent a lot of time at the hospital, and when she wasn't there, she was still under a lot of pressure and stress. She was worried and didn't smile as much. Jeff and Kristi needed relief—time to get away together.

"You always hear about such things happening in other people's families, but you never think it will happen in your own."

Chapter Thirty-seven

BROKEN BARRIERS

August 19, 1992. One year of life, a birthday gift. This birthday is celebrated against the odds, a broken barrier of time.

Even in the uncertainty of the present, Michael's one year of life has been worth the struggle a million times over. One powerless little boy's life is unquestionably worth the price paid for him a billion times and again.

But for today...a celebration in isolation.

Sterilized cake. Sterilized presents. Michael on one side; lots of balloons and family on the other. A happy day for all, especially with the news of the best gift of all: hope! Today his neutrophil, or white blood cell, counts break the barrier—570! Soon our baby will come home.

Our baby. Home.

A week later, Day +37, August 27. The first day back at school for Kamiakin teachers. I'm called out of a morning staff meeting to take a phone call from Kristi at the hospital.

"Guess what?" says the hopeful voice of a tired mother. "Our little boy can come home today!"

"No.... Really?"

Home! I'm hit again in the gut with a sledgehammer. Today!

Michael has started eating a little. His counts are now growing daily. There is no sign of infection. His bone marrow test last week showed no trace of disease—complete engraftment. To us, a complete miracle!

A Thursday afternoon, two o'clock, warm summer sun. It gives us a flashback to the day two months ago when we let go of Michael, when we placed him in sterile isolation and into God's hands.

For weeks we have longed for this moment to receive him back from God. Now the final barrier is broken. Once again we will have complete access to our child.

Kristi and I stand for the last time behind the curtain. In a peculiar way we feel as if we'll break some kind of law by walking back and picking up our baby.

An internal barrier of habit also must be broken. The nurse prompts us along: "It's okay; you can go in now."

Ever so cautiously we step across the red line and catch Michael by surprise.

"Hi, little guy!"

His big, blue eyes shout back, "Mommy, Daddy, what took you so long?"

With the first soft touch of his skin—unspeakable joy!

Touch, the precious gift of human warmth. We hug and kiss Michael. He strokes Kristi's face as if he is absorbing life itself from her skin. We hold again a little sparrow, loaned back to us with handprints from heaven.

An Interview With
Eugene Leeland
Eugene is Jeff's dad.

"It was hard when we found out about the insurance problem, but we knew we were going to figure it out one way or another. We were going to give him every chance in the world to recover.

"It was such a long period of time prior to the actual bone marrow transplant, and he was in and out of the hospital so many times. But to see what he had to go through in radiation and chemotherapy treatments prior to the transplant itself I think was the hardest part. His mouth was full of sores. And then we were isolated from him.

"We still remember him coming out of isolation, sitting in his mother's lap and touching her face because for so long there had been no contact, no skin on skin. He just couldn't keep his hands off of her; he had to touch her."

Chapter Thirty-eight

THE AFTERMATH

On August 31, as I am scrambling to prepare for the stampede of students to hit the halls of Kamiakin the next day, Faye, the secretary, phones on my intercom. "Jeff, a man is here, inquiring about coaching football. Do we need any coaches?"

"No," I say without hesitating, "everything is filled."

Our offensive coordinator had resigned in June, and with no one readily available to coach and little time to search for a replacement, I tentatively had decided to fill the position myself. But I had foolishly overcommitted myself, not knowing what the future would hold for Michael and our family. The present scenario left me without enough time and energy to perform my normal duties, let alone coach. And the instability of Michael's condition could pull me away from school at any time.

A minute later Faye calls back. "He says he would even volunteer if we need him. He's such a nice gentleman; would you want to just talk to him?"

"Okay. Send him on back to my office."

Moments later, standing before me is Shin, a Japanese

man fifty-four years old and five feet, four inches tall. "Come on in," I say. "Have a seat."

Shin is a P.E. teacher who retired from the Los Angeles City Schools and moved to the Seattle area the previous year with his wife. He tells me he lives nearby and loves coaching football. As he drove past the school, he decided to stop in and see if there were any coaching vacancies. Besides, his wife is shooing him out of the house, he jokes without smiling.

As we visit, he notices the poster on my office wall—an article with a picture of Michael and the school address for donations. He remembers hearing about our son and placing money in a canister for him at a restaurant last spring. I thank him and update him on Michael's progress, sharing also a bit of my stretch between home and work.

It finally occurs to me what's sitting in front of me. As I talk, I am privately brainstorming a way I might offer this man my coaching position.

Shin tells me his résumé and letters of recommendation are at home and asks if I would mind if he got them. A half-hour later he returns with a large envelope in hand.

Shin Matsutani. Twenty-nine years a teacher, head of the P.E. department in a junior high school of two thousand, supervisor for a P.E. staff of nine other teachers, successful coach, known as "the little general." Many favorable reviews. I scan the paperwork, quickly perceiving that he ought to be interviewing me.

"How would you feel about coaching offense?" I ask.

"First let me tell you that I prayed with my wife, Roberta," says Shin, a man of deep faith. "We feel as though the Lord has directed me here to help you. So I will coach football as your assistant, but I do not want to be paid. If they pay me, I will give it back to you. I will be your shadow here at school for the next two weeks. I will learn your job, both as athletic director and teacher. If there is any reason you need to go home, I will be your substitute. I will not substitute for anyone else, only for you."

I sit transfixed, like a child being read the beginning of a fairy tale, speechlessly absorbing every well-pronounced word. Words that begin weaving an incredible safety net beneath me for my family. Words that stun me again with the intricate detail of God's handiwork.

That day Shin becomes my angel. As time passes, his "safety net" is a promise well kept. He is everything he preached. "Be the pizza man," he would say. "You must deliver!"

Between August and March, Michael is hospitalized five times with infection—and Shin is there for me. Whenever I am called away, he delivers, helping me face mountains of details, becoming my model and mentor. Mentally tough, yet meek; demanding, yet caring. A quiet gentleman with a voice like a boom box. He is to this day a man I call "friend."

In addition to this angel at work, there is an angel at home. An angelic being in motherly form who performs around-the-clock clinical tasks of caring for Michael. For months she charts caloric intake, bandages and rebandages, flushes his Hickman line, gives medications, and operates the portable home IV pump. Through October she regularly buckles Michael into his car seat for a ride downtown to the Fred Hutchinson Outpatient Clinic for ongoing blood work and follow-up care. Kristi.

Even though Michael is home, his precious new marrow and immune system are still weak and untested. Fears and uncertainty still pierce our hearts. Will Amy's transplanted immune cells compatibly ally themselves with Michael's organs, or will they mount an attack against him in graft-versus-host disease? Will the new cells defend him from normal childhood illnesses and the upcoming flu season? Will there be any harmful consequences from receiving the mega-doses of chemotherapy and radiation? And ultimately—the sharpest dagger of all—were the leukemic cells completely destroyed?

Michael's road to recovery is not smooth. Mystery fevers and infections place detours in his path soon after discharge. On September 24 he spikes a high fever and is admitted back into Swedish Hospital. After a few days of high-powered antibiotics, he is home again.

On October 10 the fever strikes again, and X-rays reveal a spot on Michael's lung, clearly indicating some sort of respiratory infection. The exact type, unknown. Once again he is hospitalized.

The past year has been for us a crash course in microbiology and pharmacology, a self-study in tiny bugs and drugs. Of the three general categories of infection—virus, bacteria, and fungus—we have learned that the most commonly feared post-transplant fungal infection is called "aspergillus." Healthy individuals can carry a tolerable amount of fungal germs in their bodies, holding them in check with a normal immune system. But an immune system that has been depressed over a long period of time, which is inevitable in a bone marrow transplant, can allow one of these pathogens to breed uncontrollably.

Antibiotics can effectively fight bacterial infection, but not viruses or fungi. By the time the internal, mold-like aspergillus infection is discovered, it is difficult, often impossible, to treat, ending in a deadly internal takeover. We know well this heartache, as we saw a neighbor patient become a victim of this fungal enemy.

On October 19 we meet with the respiratory specialist and hear the possible prognosis, a prognosis that incites familiar fears. A CAT scan takes multiple images of Michael's infected lung. Antibiotics are prescribed in hopes the spot is a treatable bacterial infection. In ten days another CAT scan will reveal any changes in the affected area. If it grows despite medication, Michael might be opposing his final enemy.

For ten long days we wait with quivering stomachs for the test results on this spot on Michael's lung. Prayer once again becomes our only buffer against the "what ifs."

October 28. Tremendous news comes as a gift packaged in a phone call from the Hutch. The spot has entirely disappeared. We praise God with unspeakable sighs of relief.

Our marathon through the Fred Hutchinson Cancer Research Center will end as it began, in a conference with his doctors. In two days they will tell us the results from Michael's recent bone marrow biopsy, recommendations for ongoing care, and his long-term prognosis—a sort of combination post-game show and pre-season highlights as a new member in the leukemia survivors league.

October 30. Kristi and I sit in the conference room a few days after Michael's final run through the clinical circuit—the bone marrow biopsy, inspections by the physician's assistant, nutrition specialist, dentist, optometrist, and radiologist.

And now, waiting…finger-tapping…small-talking…watch-checking…waiting some more. Knowing again we must soon face our deepest fears as a doctor will read the final verdict. Hoping there will be no evidence of diseased cells left in Michael's marrow. Since Amy's marrow cells are female, they carry an easy genetic marker—two X chromosomes, which differentiate them from Michael's male, X and Y chromosomes. The percentage of female cells is the scoreboard of transplant success. Anything over 97 percent will mark a victory for Michael: It will mean Amy's good blood cells are overcoming Michael's old ones.

The doctors arrive—upbeat—and begin disclosing results of this most important test. Michael's marrow contains over 99 percent Amy's cells! Lingering male cells are likely ones that make up the bone itself. Kidneys—normal. Liver—normal. The doctor reads down the list of other organ functions—normal, normal, normal! After being braced for bad news for so long, good news sneaks around behind us and pushes us in an opposite ditch of disbelief, numbness, and finally joy.

The doctor's demeanor this day is, at best, an expression of cautious optimism. For Michael, the future holds distant hopes and nearly certain side effects from a two-faced friend, chemoradiotherapy. Sterility, typically a given, will be tested for in his teens. Growth delays and hormonal treatments—highly probable. Arthritis in the hips, secondary tumors, behavior disorders—quite possible. Houseplants, pets, swimming pools, and crowds of people—on a list of taboos for one year.

Prognosis for the disease itself follows a law of diminishing returns. One year post-transplant is critical, the greatest chance of relapse. Two years, a landmark. If the disease is still in remission by August 1994, Michael has a 95 percent probability of a lifetime cure. Remission for five years would mean he's cured.

Five years is a distant horizon, a long road ahead. But in our eyes, he is healthy *today*. We are not in denial of impending possibilities, dreadful possibilities. Rather we are constructing the defense of a grateful spirit to keep the phantoms of anxiety at bay, phantoms that would steal the treasure of God's blessing today.

Thank You, God, he's home. Our sparrow is home.

An Interview With
Kristi Leeland
Kristi is Michael's mom.

"It was both encouraging and heart-wrenching to interact with other parents and patients on the floor, to hear how well they were doing or how some of the kids weren't doing well at all. That was especially hard for me. I got to know a woman from back east whose little boy was the same age as Michael. He didn't make it. When you get close to the parents and you watch their kids go downhill, that's hard.

"I still think about those parents whose kids didn't make it. Why our child and not theirs? I don't understand it. God must have some plans for Michael—but I'm not saying He didn't have plans for their children. I don't know. All we knew was that these children, too, were precious in God's sight. I know that our Lord loves children even more than we parents love them, but that didn't make it easy. I placed myself in their shoes. I think it was a way of preparing myself...just in case."

Chapter Thirty-nine

REFLECTIONS: ONE YEAR LATER

August, 1993. One year since Michael was released into our arms again. We've settled back into a common place. At day's end we tuck our flock of little ones into bed, being careful to say our good-night prayers: "We thank You so much, dear God...." It's an often recurring theme in our home these days.

Kristi crawls in bed early, too, tired from her labors of love. I stay up to take advantage of the quiet moments of solitude for a special work of my own. This particular evening I reflect upon the recent portraits of our handsome two-year-old boy.

And such pictures! Pictures with the attraction of a Caribbean isle—his bright, blue eyes and sun-washed, sandy blond hair and a smile that bathes our hearts in love.

These pictures again prompt tears of deep gratitude for treasured moments since the day Michael returned to us from his sterile sanctuary. Seeing our baby's first steps. Hearing his first words and the creak of a rocking chair in a once-silent baby's room. Feeling the touch of his soft skin and the warmth of a gentle kiss. Sharing Christmas as a family. Watching happy brothers and sisters playing on the floor.

I think about how Michael has crept through normal toddlerhood in the year gone by. No more IV's. No more transfusions. Since January, no more Hickman line. He's begun to explore, climbing and emptying everything from the fireplace to the kitchen cupboards. Even ash tracks on the carpet are a source of joy when they are the marks of a healthy, curious child.

Each day has dawned as a celebration of life. Each has brought an array of blessings, great and small. A tremendous one came when we received a letter from the Fred Hutchinson Cancer Research Center dated July 28, 1993:

> We are pleased to see Michael and his family back in the Outpatient Department for his long-term follow-up evaluation. It is gratifying to see that he continues to be in complete remission now more than one year post-transplant with documented donor engraftment.... Bone marrow aspiration showed normal cellularity with...no signs of disease relapse.

We are elated with Michael's newest report! But with the relief of burdens also comes a test of faith. The days of jubilation can relax our grip on the hope which anchored us in the hours of desperation. In reflection we keep a firm grip on the Author of such a hope.

God was not surprised when we received the call to move from Omak. Nor did He lose sight of us in the shadows of a large city.

From the first days of Michael's diagnosis to the long, anxious walks through hospital hallways, we sensed He, too, had a tear in His eye. His tender hand of mercy cradled our sick baby and soothed the spirits of our family. We held tightly to the belief that not one ounce of pain goes to waste in His hands. Somehow, as we placed it there, He molded our pain into hope.

His eye was intently watching when our broken sparrow dropped through the cracks of a manmade system. And His hand was seen as He, who long ago turned a young boy's lunch into a feast for five thousand, took a mere $60 and miraculously multiplied it into $220,000 in four short weeks.

But when our boy was journeying through the valley of the shadow of death during his transplant, then we no longer felt God's hand. It was then we felt His heartbeat. It was then we realized most deeply that He is a personal God who weeps, who is acquainted with every sorrow, who has ached with our every pain.

Finally, God's compassion was powerfully pictured through the sacrificial gift of a little girl. In her garden-like moment of decision, Amy agonizingly chose to offer what no one else could. Only her blood could remove the wall of separation between this father and his child. Through Amy's love, Michael lives. Her blood became his new life.

My reflections take me back to a familiar Bible verse I learned as a child, now viewed through the lens of the past two years. Here's my paraphrase of John 3:16:

> Our heavenly Father loved His isolated, sin-sick, spiritually dying children in the world so much that He sent and bore the agony of separation from His only begotten Son, Jesus, who shed His *perfectly matched* lifeblood for them all. So that now, whoso- ever of these children will commit their very lives

into the hands of this gracious Great Physician—
One who has offered His services as a free gift!—will
be born again with new spiritual life and be reconciled to the arms of their loving Father in heaven
who longs to embrace them, a Father who has a
homecoming prepared for them beyond description!

Truly, this is the greatest story ever told.

An Interview With
Steve Mezich
*Steve is the principal at Kamiakin Junior High School
and Jeff's good friend.*

"To this day we can hardly believe it all happened. When we started school last fall, we had a reception for Jeff and Michael in the field house with more than a thousand kids and adults in attendance. It was an opportunity to give both kids and parents an update on Michael's condition.

"At a very dramatic time in the program, the lights dimmed and a spotlight hit Michael, lying in Jeff's arms at the back of the gym. It was clear he was very alert, alive, and well.

"The kids must have clapped for fifteen minutes straight. There wasn't a dry eye in the house."

Chapter Forty

PROJECTIONS:
THE FULL CIRCLE

October 14, 1994. There was no school today, so Dameon and I went golfing. He's a high school student now, but we still get together from time to time, usually to hit a bucket of balls at the driving range. From the imaginary "whiffle ball" pro tour he plays in his backyard to the computerized version at school, Dameon is a true student of the game. But these were to be his first steps on a real golf course.

Dameon was standing anxiously in his driveway when I drove up. "I've waited a long time for this," he said as I put his clubs in the trunk of my car.

It was quite a game. Dameon sank a twelve-foot putt and perfected his Jack Nicklaus wave. But best of all, his eyes lit up with a newfound joy. After playing three holes in two hours we were given a rain check by the course manager (our game is to be continued).

But the highlight of my day came later as a three-year-old boy was riding in the car with me. "Michael, guess who I went golfing with this morning?" I asked.

"Who?"

"Dameon. Do you know who Dameon is?"

"Dameon gave his money for me."

"That's right, Michael; he did. He helped save your life!"

I was a bit surprised by this little guy's comprehension. Two weeks ago Michael sat in the pew with his mom as I spoke at Jeanne Robb's church in Shelton, Faith Lutheran. Our family went to meet and give thanks to these loved ones. There, too, I shared the story of Dameon's donation which began Michael's fund.

"Yeah, I was sick!" he said, likely recalling my words instead of his pain.

"But you're all better now, aren't you?"

"Uh-huh."

"Michael, someday do you want to help people, too? Maybe you can help some kids who are sick?"

"Yeah, I can help, too," he said in a grown-up voice.

Now, over two years post-transplant (although still two years away from being pronounced "cured"), Michael remains in complete remission. Each passing day brings brighter hopes for more tomorrows, but still we must live just for today. And despite early tests that indicated his body was not producing any growth hormone, Michael has continued to grow normally. After a recent check-up, Michael's specialist admitted to Kristi, "I'm stumped. I have no explanation!" The gleam in Kristi's eyes, as she told me the doctor's response, radiated the joy of an answered prayer.

Now Michael's words are the last, small links needed to complete the full circle of love, the circle Jesus spoke of when He said, "It is more blessed to give than to receive."

And perhaps Michael will be one, like Dameon, to pass along the debt of love. Perhaps, by God's grace, Michael's story will continue.

Chapter Forty-one

CLASSROOMS OF COMPASSION

*Even though I gave him all of my money
I was just a pebble on a big beach.
I am proud of what I did,
But it's more about what we all did.*

DAMEON SHARKEY,
JUANITA HIGH SCHOOL NEWSPAPER

The gifts of the Kamiakin students were mere raindrops in our ocean of need. But it was their lightning-like spirit of compassion that electrified the community and unlocked the floodgates of grace for Michael. And now, through the Sparrow Foundation, their heart-gifts have become seed money for many more small sparrows—sixteen since 1996:

Jordan, Denise, and Kristine.
Nathan, Fiona, Kristina, and Kressa.
Jonathan, Joshua, Matthew, and Michelle.
Tiffany, Tyler, Michael, and Mikayla.
And now RJ.

Somehow the contributions these kids at Kamiakin made returned to them in boomerang form. Their class earned an unprecedented $1.1 million in scholarships when they graduated from Juanita High School in 1995. The next year Dameon, too, graduated with honors and attended Seattle Community College in woodworking. His sixty-dollar gift returned to him as a six-hundred-dollar scholarship for six straight terms.

And now, through the Sparrow Foundation, thousands more young people across the nation have become catalysts of the same spirit of compassion and contribution in their own communities by adopting the causes of those sparrows above:

- Shelton High School, Antioch Bible Church youth, and numerous church groups in Illinois
- Kamiak High School
- Endeavor Elementary School
- Tyler Texas Girl Scouts
- Arvada Colorado Rainbow Girls
- Lake Placid Middle School Fellowship of Christian Athletes
- Malone College "Helping Hands"
- Bellarmine Prep's football team
- Kent Middle School and PTSA
- Hilliard Middle & Senior High Fellowship of Christian Athletes
- Missoula Youth for Christ

And finally, Bellermine Prep students piloted the first-ever Sparrow Club on their Tacoma, Washington campus.

These students have created a future model for classrooms of compassion. So far, they have adopted two kids from Children's Hospital in Seattle.

The Sparrow Foundation, birthed from Michael's fund, is a young people's charity. As a 501(c) 3 nonprofit corporation, its mission is to empower kids and teens to reach out in a spirit of compassion and contribution to help children in medical need.

A Letter From
JORDAN WEST
*Jordan was a captain of the Bellermine Prep football team
and a member of the Sparrow Club.*

In May of 1998 our coach spoke to us about the Sparrow Foundation and how it financially helps sick children and their families. Matthew Randall was a boy with cancer, and it was proposed to us that we could help him and his family. Everyone jumped at the chance and immediately began to think of ways we could raise money.

One way we decided to raise money was by having a senior football player auction. This included people bidding on each player; in turn we would be servants for a day. The big money-raiser, however, happened one Saturday afternoon. A bunch of us got together and decided to have a car wash for Matthew. Four hours went by and the money rolled in.

After the auction, the car wash, and a company matching our money, the total amount came to over five thousand dollars! We were so happy and knew the Randalls would be even happier.

The look on Mrs. Randall's face when we presented what we had done made us all realize why we had done this. They could not believe what we had done for them, and it made each of us feel so awesome inside.

The experience Matthew gave us all will never be forgotten. Here was a little boy who was fighting for his life, and though he may not have realized all the complications, all he cared about was playing with his new friends. He showed us all what really matters in life: It's not about the cards you're dealt; it's about how you play the hand. Matthew has been through more in his few short years than most people go through in a lifetime. I thank him for being a role model to me, and I thank the Lord for allowing him to live such a beautiful life by showing what it really means to live.

Chapter Forty-two

HEAVEN'S HANDPRINTS

January 4, 1999. It's 6 P.M. I'm home after work. I've taken a job with a publishing company in central Oregon to support my directorship of the Sparrow Foundation. Michael, now seven, is on my lap, clicker in hand. I bounce him on my knees as we watch TV. together. Three-year-old Andrew, the latest addition to the Leeland family, is happily playing on the floor with his toys.

"Wow, Mike—your muscles are getting big." I squeeze his biceps.

Then, on Michael's upper arm, I feel a knot—a lump half the size of a golf ball under his muscle. Hmm. With a growing uneasiness in my stomach, I call Kristi into the room.

"Kristi, come and feel this."

A year-and-a-half past his five-year remission threshold, Michael—a high-energy, big-sister-teasing, quick-witted, multi-sport-playing second grader—has been called *cured*. He, too, has also been spared many of the more tragic consequences of a bone marrow transplant—and spreads his wings like most seven-year-olds, cancer-free. Recovery is, however, less the victory celebration than some expect. Rather it's more of a tippy-toe, look-over-the-shoulder escape from enemy territory. And Michael bears his share of battle scars.

I sense Kristi's heart sink inside her as she feels the lump on him.

"We need to get this checked tomorrow."

January 6. Michael's arm was X-rayed yesterday. It was a tumor on the bone of his upper right arm—probably the fallout from past barrages of chemo and total body radiation. Dr. Svendsen made an appointment for Michael next Thursday at Shriner's Children's Hospital in Portland, Oregon. The pediatric tumor specialist will likely remove the lump after an examination.

Michael has learned to take things in stride. He's grown accustomed to his regular six-month follow-ups. He learned to accept the KOMO TV news camera at his every birthday party up to his fifth. He's absorbed his medical history quite well. But now he's carrying a new kind of burden—the mental and emotional capacity to care about his future "what ifs."

It's 9 A.M. Home school Bible lesson time. Michael and Andrew are Kristi's only students this year. Kevin is a fourth grader at Evergreen Elementary. Amy is an eighth grader at Hugh Hartman Middle School. Jaclyn is a junior at Redmond High.

"Today's Bible lesson, boys," Kristi says, "is from 1 Peter 5:7: 'Cast all your cares on the Lord, for He cares for you.'" Kristi continues, teaching Michael and Andrew what it means to trust God. She finishes by asking, "Michael, what does it mean for you to trust God right now?"

After a brief hesitation, Michael replies, "Well, I can put

'Mr. Lump' in Jesus' hands. Then I don't have to worry anymore."

Yesterday, I was filled with anxiety as I prayed; "Lord, help us, heal Michael." And then, "God, what would You have me learn from this?"

Today, Michael became my teacher. And here, in one simple statement of childike faith, we are pointed to the place to rest our case when "lumpike" nerves knot up inside us.

January 12. Yes, Michael put Mr. Lump in good hands. It was molded into a benign tumor, a callouslike mass of soft tissue. And our fears were molded into a powerful lesson from a seven-year-old about what it means to trust God.

Relieved and rejoicing, we again see the handprints of heaven on Michael's life—lumps and all.

An Interview With
Michael

Q: "Michael, can you tell me about your story?"
A: "Jesus saved my life."
Q: "How did he do that?"
A: "He gave me Amy's blood so that I could live."
Q: "What else did He do for you?"
A: "He gave me His blood so I can go to heaven."

THE SPARROW
FOUNDATION

The Sparrow Foundation is a nonprofit, charitable, educational organization. It was birthed to keep alive the spirit of grace that inspired the Kamiakin Junior High community to reach out to Michael Leeland. This foundation has already become a catalyst for several similar efforts by establishing a process for schools, youth organizations, service clubs, and churches to do service projects for children with medical needs.

The compassion of just one neighbor can be a most powerful medicine for the brokenhearted, and the collective caring of a community is a most blessed kind of insurance. We pray this legacy of love will continue, and perhaps one day more young people will be able to say, like Dameon, "It was the greatest thing I ever did."

For more information, please write:

The Sparrow Foundation

P.O. Box 77752

Seattle, WA 98177

www.sparrow-fdn.org